THE "NEW-AGE"
AMERICA
& PRESIDENT TRUMP'S
INVISIBLE
POLITICS

IN WORLD GOVERNANCE
(The Future & the SECURITY of You & I)

THE "NEW-AGE"
AMERICA
& PRESIDENT TRUMP'S
INVISIBLE
POLITICS

IN WORLD GOVERNANCE
(The Future & the SECURITY of You & I)

Stephen B. Oladipo, Ph.D

ARPress
ILLUMINATING IDEAS
EMPOWERING VOICES

ARPress
45 Dan Road Suite 5
Canton MA 02021
Hotline: 1(888) 821-0229
Fax: 1(508) 545-7580

Ordering Information:

Quantity sales. Special discounts are available on quantity purchases by corporations, associations, and others. For details, contact the publisher at the address above.

Printed in the United States of America.

ISBN-13:   Softcover   979-8-89330-519-7

              eBook   979-8-89330-520-3

Library of Congress Control Number: 2024901012

Table Of Contents

LIST OF PICTURES

DEDICATION

He understands the course of men and provides the way through the deepest waters. You have been there again like always. To God and only True God for everything I have been through in the journey of reckoning.

Heather Hope, 2018.

ACKNOWLEDGEMENTS

I will start with the communities that made available to me the space and the resource support throughout the process that led to the accomplishment of this great policy review piece. These include: Flossmoor, Matteson and Oak forest communities in the Illinois South Suburbs.

It is also a privilege for me to have the rare opportunity to appreciate the Christian Communities and faith-based organizations that enhanced my capacity all through the period of this historic work. The list include: Flossmoor Community Church, Hutchison, Flossmoor; Infant Jesus of Prague, Flossmoor; The Episcopal Church of St. John the Evangelist, Park Drive, Flossmoor; St. Lawrence O'Toole, Matteson and; Redeemer Lutheran Church, Oak Forest. They are all in South Suburbs, Illinois.

I thanked specific individuals that have personally shown concerns in my journey to accomplishing this. Principal among these individuals are: Rev. Scott Oberle of First Congregation Church, Downers Grove; Dr. Mrs. Brenda Roberson, New Faith Baptist Church; Ms. Margaret Epperson, Flossmoor; Mrs. Gail C., St. Lawrence O'Toole; Brother John Harvey of Korean United; Ms. Myrtle Jackson of Excel into Independence; Mr. & Mrs. Bell & Iris Bestow; Rev. Sellars Vines and Mrs. Joyce Coleman: both of New Faith Baptist Church, Matteson, Illinois.

The list continues with the following individuals whom life crosses our paths at some critical moments: Ms. Doreen Nnaemeka, MN; Ms. Clare George (The Grandma), MN; Mr. Brian Kendall (A very unique man I once met), MN Ms. MAE, MN and; Ms. Elizabeth of AME Church, St. Paul, MN.

Still on the list of individuals to be recognized; Pastor (Mrs.) Olabisi Suleodu & her amiable family; Deacon Bada Olatunde & family; Pastor (Mrs.) Sodeinde Victoria; Ms. Esho (RCCG, Lancaster church secretary); Dr. Reni Adebayo-Ige (Antelope Valley College); Mr. Kehinde Augustine & his lovely family; Mr. Sunday Olowokere & family; Mr. Collins Olurinde Akinsola; Jadesola Obadeyi (California State University, Northridge); Lisa Dunn & family; Dorothy Moshood

(Washington State); Vera Ekeka (TX); Uchey Oluwakemi Anogwum; Mr. Adebayo & family; Shirley Teague (GA); Pastor Kelvin (River Bible Church, Beverly, MA); Ms. Roxanne and Rita S. Corbeit (Both of River Bible Church, Beverly, MA); Joyce Eyen, MA; and the Late Angela Tyler of blessed memory.

I cannot forget you my adopted Uncle: Dr. Solibe Ufondu (PA). Somehow, life occasioned our path to cross through the mystery only destiny can explain. Ever since, you have been more to me like a relation. Thank you.

Somehow, certain individual will register a name on the list such as this, despite the nature of contribution life occasioned from their end in the course of time and process of development. Titilola Joseph is recognized equally.

List of Abbreviations

CBS:	Columbia Broadcasting System
CIA:	Central Intelligence Agency
DACA:	Deferred Action for Childhood Arrivals
DHS:	Department of Homeland Security
DMZ:	Demilitarized Zone
DPRK:	Democratic People's Republic of Korea
EAD:	Employment Authorization Document
EPA:	Environmental Protection Agency
E.U:	European Union
EEZ:	Exclusive Economic Zone
FBI:	Federal Bureau of Investigation
GMDAC:	Global Migration Data Analysis Centre GOP
H.R:	House of Representatives
IAEA:	International Atomic Energy Agencies.
INA:	Immigration and Nationality Act (INA)
ICRC:	International Committee of the Red Cross
IOM:	International Organization for Migration
MFP:	Money, Fame & Product
NPT:	Non-Proliferation Treaty
NPT:	Nuclear Proliferation Treaty
TRO:	Temporary restraining order
US:	United States
USRAP:	U.S. Refugee Admissions Program
UN:	United Nations
UNHCR:	United Nations High Commission for Refugees
WHO:	World Health Organization

- "AMERICA . . . (THE DREAMED LAND) WHERE CHILDREN ARE IN CONTROL OF THEIR PARENTS . . . WHERE DOES THE FUTURE LIES WITH A GENERATION WITHOUT MORAL VALUES BUT GUN & GANG CULTURE?" Stephen B. Oladipo

- "THE WAY TO TOMORROW IS TODAY: THERE WILL BE NO SPECIAL MAGIC ABOUT THE OUTLOOK OF TOMORROW OUTSIDE THE PLANS OF TODAY AROUND IT." Stephen B. Oladipo

- THE ULTIMATE MEASURE OF A MAN IS NOT WHERE HE STANDS IN MOMENTS OF COMFORT AND CONVENIENCE, BUT WHERE HE STANDS AT TIMES OF CHALLENGE AND CONTROVERSY." Martin Luther King Jr.

- "AN ARTIST MUST BE FREE TO CHOOSE WHAT HE DOES, CERTAINLY, BUT HE MUST ALSO NEVER BE AFRAID TO DO WHAT HE MUST CHOOSE." Langston Hughes

- "I HAVE LEARNED OVER THE YEARS THAT WHEN ONE'S MIND IS MADE UP, THIS DIMINISHES FEAR; KNOWING WHAT MUST BE DONE DOES AWAY WITH FEAR." Rosa Parks

- "TIME CHANGES WEATHER. BEHAVIORAL PATTERN CHANGES RELATIONSHIP. HUMAN DEVELOPMENT CHANGES THE LAWS; JUST AS THE NEED FOR PEACE & SAFETY CHANGES THE RULES." Stephen B. Oladipo

CHAPTER ONE

1.0   INTRODUCTION

Those who live to see tomorrow defines itself can only accept whatever tomorrow gives to them. Unfortunately, not many of such people, nations and generations possess the well-without to deal with the consequences of their past inactions. Many nations around the world today are languishing in poverty, fear, terror, insurgence, economic depression and misfortunes of all kinds because they did nothing when their yesterday was about to produce the future they may not have the capacity to deal with. Like the economists projected: 'micro activities always aggregate to macro activities.' This implies that if individuals within a household, a nation or generation refuse to think right, the aggregate results may equally disappoint them. Accumulations of wrong decisions by individuals, group of individuals or national(s) of a nation will eventually equate the reality of their future direction. This preamble should speak volumes in the minds of millions of American-citizens who in the interest of politics of the moment and sentimental opinions are yet to open their eyes unto the realities of prevailing happenings around the world so as to be able to take control of their own nation rather than being careless in the season of carefulness. Otherwise, the great America may also toe the path where its internal insecurity becomes pathology. Where the enemies within its borders may distract it from its socio-economic, developmental and overall leadership roles. Where its men and women within the law enforcement sector will be exposed to higher challenges in keeping the communities safe. Where the normal daily routing of the ordinary citizen may be hampered due to unsafe environment. Where hanging out in public places may become dreaded and, where extra vigilance may have to be placed on all transportation routes: ranging from local airports to bus stations. Where complexity may become the order of the day through catastrophic insurgent activities. These are the least imagined situations, on the list of what careless and un-proactive measures towards taking charge of America now may accrue to the nation's future. Lest, the great America becomes the laughing stock of its enemies once more, like it happened during September, 11. Lest, America opens its own treasury to the looters of its souls through unrealistic and emotional decisions. Lest, America as well amass its own troubles through lack of sensitivity to the rhythm of this dispensation. Lest, America incurs the likes of precarious insecurity situations which are already bedeviling many other prominent and previously serene countries (even) within the western hemisphere. Only the wise, they say, learns from the front to avoid the experience of common-tribulations.

Loudly or silently, another 'MOVEMENT' has begun from the leading nation of the world to the rest of it. Never in the history of America has there been an administrative overhauling of a new government to undo the activities of immediate past predecessor(s). Never has America, the 'BILL-PAYER' antagonized the rest of the world in a united assembly called the UN. Never in history has America reviewed her spending in the projects and developmental activities of other nations against the benefits it stands to derive from such nations. Even though, there is no free-food in international politics they say. However, hate it or like it, the 45th President of America, Donald J. Trump is walking away from the status quo. He is challenging the establishments both in America and around the world and, orchestrating a 'force of change' which is the enemy of status quo. Politically, economically, socio-welfare wise and on the ground of religion-stand, there is an on-going movement away from the status quo; a force of change many historians are yet to catalogue on the shelf of relativity. America and Americans have never been this 'half and half.' There has been war of words among the pros and the cons. There have been open confrontations to policies that challenged the 'major-interests.' There have been movements against presidential fiats that trampled upon many individuals' areas of business-interest among other fight-backs and collusions to stop the 'hand' that reaches to recreate a new dawn in the land of America.

As a sociological reviewer and an opinionist, I may not possess the political capacity to adjudge this locomotor-movement or the verdicts of the 45th President on issues of immigration, taxation, religion-ethics, security, economy, international relations, international dispositions, media-antagonism and/or politics but I am confident of one constant factor; the world of tomorrow may not forget President Donald J. Trump in a hurry. Beyond the border of hatred and acrimony, his legacy may live longer than the story that brought him into power. His memory may last longer than the history of the preceding forty four (44) leaders. If the theory is anything to go by, which posits; no man champions a change and remains obscured in the history of time and reference. I have no doubts; the world of tomorrow will harbor the landmarks of these policy-measures, even though, one man may be the sacrifice.

The subsequent pages of this book will carefully attempt a review of President Donald J. Trump's administrative policies in the light of realistic events of today, while thematically analyzing the major issues under discourse without the temptation of self-interest, subjectivity, parochialism or provincialism. Expect an objective review without fear of persecution.

CHAPTER TWO

2.0 AMERICAN PRESIDENTS AND CHALLENGES OF ACCUSATIONS: FROM GEORGE WASHINGTON TO DONALD J. TRUMP

In the history of leadership in America, most past presidents have not had it so smooth in the course of their administrations. Several of them have been accused on several things. They have all had issues to deal with. Some of these issues had ranged from personality-attacks to image battery. Some have had it rough with women; others have been blemished on foreign-military roles. Some have had their family-life insulted; others have struggled with identity questions while the new age insurgent activities around the world have equally occasioned a few other leaders in America to take policy measures that have alienated them from the receptive nature of their people. Summarily, no presidency has ever had it so clean from the ploys of accusations and/or politically motivated troubles to un-focus or unseats them. For instance, President Barrack Obama (2009 – 2017), the 44th President of the United States, was troubled on issues relating identity for the most years in his first tenure as a President of the United States. When suddenly, it was alleged Obama was not a-US-born citizen. His political antagonists claimed he was born in Kenya. This claim was even traced back to sources close to Barrack Obama himself. In Newby (2012)'s narratives, Obama had an agent named: Acton & Dystel who published a promotional booklet in 1991 that stated that Obama was born in Kenya. Unfortunately, the claim that Obama was a Kenya-born lasted on the agent's web platform till 2007. To worse matters, Obama's political oppositions tracked speeches and further information from literary agents which linked statements such as: "Kenya is Obama's homeland" to Michelle Obama (Pollak, 2012). The seriousness of this matter was that it is unconstitutional to have a foreign born citizen to be the President of the United States. Since Kenya was still British colony as at 1961 when Obama was born. By virtue of this situation, Obama's father was argued to be a British subject and likewise Obama. Consequently, Obama's political antagonists argued on this citizenship-status premise to keep his presidency busy with investigative activities during his time. Aside other re-occurring socio-economic, religion and terrorism questions he had had to confront during his reign.

During the presidency of George W. Bush (2001 – 2009) as the 43rd President of the United States; all sorts of investigative activities came up to run him out of office. Many political analysts have alleged that most of the investigative activities advanced against Bush's presidency were largely from some opposition-politicians who cared to see him impeached at all cost. Some of the probing investigations against his administration had occasioned many impeachable charges been brought to the floor of the House of Representatives' committee on judiciary. One of such disturbing moments under his tenure was on 10th June, 2008 when congressmen introduced about 35 articles of impeachment against him on the floor of the US House of Representatives. The congressmen involved in that particular impeachment move included: Dennis Kucinich with another co-sponsor named: Robert Wexler. The impeachable charges tabled against him were voted upon by members of the house before resolution was referred to the Judiciary committee the following day (Anthony, 2008).

A list of the allegations and accusations against Bush's presidency included: (i) His roles in Iraq war or Iraq invasion (ii) His Valerie Plame, CIA agent's affair (iii) His roles in creating likely war situation for Iran (iv) His approach to capturing and treatment of prisoners of war (v) His accusation on spying and wiretapping within the United States of America (vi) His failure to comply with congressional subpoenas (vii) His activities during 2004 elections (viii) His attitude /policy on global warming (ix) Accusations on his failure to respond to prior intelligence on September 11 terrorist attack of twin towers and the aftermath of that insurgent attack (x) His falsification of numbers of US troop's death and injuries among other accusations and allegations.

William Jefferson Clinton (1993 – 2001), the 42nd President of the United States popularly known as Bill Clinton. In his own case, four different women publicly accused him of sexual harassment or assault. In fact, one of the women categorically accused him of rape. Juanita Broaddrick launched the worse missile against Clinton's reputation when she accused him of raping her in 1978. That was the period Clinton was the attorney general in Arkansa. According to Relman (2017), Broadrick was a middle age woman of about 35 years of age, serving as the administrator in a nursing home. Her encounter with Clinton took place during Clinton's campaign stop at her nursing home. The brief meeting lead to an agreed appointment between the two to meet each other at a coffee shop within a hotel. In Broadrisk's first public reportage of this incident to a news line regarded as Buzzfeed News, she claimed Clinton rather came into her hotel room instead of the coffee arena. There and then, what Broadrisk described as violent rape took place within the hotel room. In fact, in her claims, Clinton bloodied her lip by biting it.

According to Washington post, two of the lady's associates corroborated this story by airing their knowledge of the affair between the duo. Another allegation close to this is Kathleen Willey's story. According to Kathleen, as reported by Relman (2017), Clinton kissed and fondled her breasts. Kathleen was said to be a volunteer within the White House at this period while the incident took place during a meeting in the Oval office in 1993 where the lady claimed Clinton forced her to touch his crotch. Before this alleged incident, Clinton and Willey were said to have had a discussion about the financial difficulties Willey and her husband were having at the period. Willey was alleged to have sought Clinton's assistance for a job-transition from volunteer position to paying job within the white house so as to be able to get out of her family financial issues. It was on this premise Clinton was sympathetic and asked to speak with her in one of the rooms within the palace. That was the room where Willey claimed Clinton cornered her and sexually harassed her.

Next is the Paula Jones's story. This was another woman who accused Clinton of sexual harassment. Jones was a former Arkansas state employee. She claimed to have incurred sexual harassment from the 42nd President of America during a government quality management conference that had Clinton in attendance. Bill Clinton was still a governor at this period. In the words of Jones, captured by Mathews (2016), a state police officer approached her and courteously informed her that Bill Clinton, the governor wanted to meet her. She was in the company of the police man who eventually lead her straight to the hotel room at Little-rock where Clinton lodged. In Matthews' (2016) narration, this was the hotel room where Jones claimed Clinton proposed sex to her and revealed his genital to arouse her. Jones claimed she rejected the sex offer because she was not that type of girl. But Clinton rushed over her before she could grab the door and walk out. According to Jones, when she was leaving the room after the harassment, she noticed the police outside the hotel room smirking. This incident occurred in 1991 but Jones made it public in 1994 after which she advanced a lawsuit against Clinton on Sexual-harassment. After the initial dismissal and re-appealing on this case however, Jones got $850,000 from Clinton as part of out-of-court settlement deal. Though Clinton did not admit guilt or apologize to Jones (Matthews, 2016).

The next case was with Leslie Millwee. Leslie was a former television reporter. She claimed her sexual-assault experience with Clinton dated back to 1980. This was the same period while Clinton was still the governor of Arkansas.

According to her, in Matthew's (2016) report, Clinton groped her on many occasions at her television station, which is now-defunct. She claimed to have had Clinton followed her into her editing studio on several occasions. She claimed Clinton usually came up behind her in the small studio-room rubbing her shoulders and running his hands through to her breasts. Leslie also claimed this incident got escalated in the course of time. She alleged Clinton now hunched her to the points where he usually had orgasms. The woman claimed the reason she did not report the incident at the time was because Clinton was still the Governor of the state and she was equally worried about the consequences of her coming forward to report the incident (Matthews, 2016).

To describe the veracity of these accusations and offences against President Jefferson Clinton in his days, these sexual harassment issues almost cost Bill Clinton his Presidency since the Democrats were trying to save the image of the party rather than going down with him. Specifically, on 19th December, 1998 the House of Representatives approved two articles of impeachment against President Jefferson Clinton, one for perjury and the other for obstruction of justice. He was in this struggle for almost two months before the Senate could come to his rescue on 12th February, 1999 and acquitted him of the alleged offences.

With President George H. W. Bush (1989 –1993) the 41st President of America, it was the battle of women harassment. Under his Presidency, five more women came up with accusation of buttocks' groping after actress Heather Lind's accusation of sexual harassment. President H.

W. Bush's list of accusers included: Rosalyn Corrigan, Christina Baker, Jordana Grolnick among others who narrated their stories to batter H. W. Bush's public image.

According to Michal (2017), a woman who chose to protect her identity by being anonymous had reported H. W. Bush to CNN on accusation of groping. The woman claimed the former President H. W. Bush grabbed her buttocks in the course of shifting closer to him during a photo session with

H. W. Bush and her father. This, she claimed, happened in 1992 during a campaign event in Dearborn, Michigan. Rosalyn Corrigan, traced her own experience with H. W. Bush back to 2003 when she was still a teenager (16 years old). Corrigan claimed to have encountered Bush at a gathering of CIA officers since one of her parents who was a CIA member brought her along to the gathering. In her report of H. W. Bush to Time Newspapers, she claimed that the 79 years old W. Bush as at the time grabbed her from behind as she posed for a photo with him and her mother. She claimed W. Bush only dropped his hands from her waist after roughening his hands down to her buttocks with a tender ripe squeeze while the photographer was busy counting down from one to three before snapping the picture. Christina Baker Kline is another woman; a novelist who also came forward with her own accusation. In her claims, H. W. Bush harassed her too during a photo session. According to her, Bush whispered into her ears in the course of the photo-arrangement, asking her if she knows his favorite book. While simultaneously squeezing his hands through her buttocks, she claimed. New York, East Hamptons made a news story out of this with Mark Saglioco, using Getty images. Jordana Grolnick was also listed on this list of H.W. Bush's harassment on women. The New York actress (Grolnick) reported her own groping experience with

W. Bush to Deadspin. According to her, this took place during a photo session "while we all circle around Barbara and W. Bush for a photo. He reached his hands around me from behind and roughened his hands through my waist as the group smiled to the photographer in the pose" (Michal, 2017). Usually, aside the media insults H. W. Bush incured, individual name-calling that tend to paint the former president as a dirty old man lingered on these reportages. This issue and chronic others confronted the public image of former President H. W. Bush during and after his tenure of office as the President of the United States.

Ronald Wilson Reagan (1981-1989) was the 40th President of the United States of America. His presidency was equally said to have experienced scandalous allegations. Under his tenure, about 138 administrative officials were investigated, indicted and convicted. This was alleged to be the biggest investigative activities conducted on an America President's administration and, equally the largest number of conviction so far under a presidential tenure (Brinkley, 2009). The worse political damage was done to his presidency in November 1986 when Reagan conceded to the allegation of selling weapons to the Islamic Republic of Iran. It was also known that the large chunk of the money made through Iran arm deal was channeled into funding the right-wing Contras counter-revolutionary organizations, which seek to overthrow the government of Nicaragua; the socialist Sandinista. Another scandal under Reagan administration was through the Environmental Protection Agency (EPA) where more than twenty top employees were sacked from office within the first three years of his administration. The official's offence largely bothered on the release of super fund grants to favor the Republican Party's candidates who sought elections into local offices at the time. Some of those top EPA officials were charged with misuse of public fund (superfund) and they were convicted of perjury.

Another key problem with Reagan administration was the popular: "Reagan's 'elimination of loopholes" through tax code which lead to savings and loan crisis. The crisis has been alleged as the largest financial scandal in the history of the United States among others, which included operation III wind. Operation III wind was the 1986 investigation into the corruption of the military official and private defense contractors by the Federal Bureau of Investigation (FBI) (Johnson, 2003).

The list continues with: James Earl Carter, Jr. (1977-1981), the 39th President of the United States of America who was more popular with the name: "Jimmy" Carter. Despite his many accomplishments, Polls of historians and political scientists have continuously ranked Carter as a below average president (Lavender, 2015). His lack of solution to the "stagflation" economic situation of his time berated him in the opinion of his critics. Other crisis that equally pervaded his tenure of office included: the Iran hostage crisis; the energy crisis of 1979; the invasion of the Soviet Afghanistan; the mile Island nuclear accident. He was also criticized for his boycott of the 1980 International Summer Olympics in Moscow (Lavender, 2015).

Next is Gerald Rudolph Ford (1974-1977), the 38th President of America. According to Cannon (2006) "President Gerald Rudolph Ford was the only man in history to serve as president and vice president (of the United States) without being elected to either positions." Aside his involvement in Vietnam war, Ford was critically criticized for presiding over the worst economy in the last four decades of American history since the Great Depression. In his period, there was soaring growing inflation and serious economic recession (Frum, 2000).

Richard Milhous Nixon (1969-1974) was the 37th American President who was politically tagged as the worse President America ever produced. He was also recorded as the only American President till date who has resigned from office (William, 2016). Among other criticisms, his administration was belittled as such which generally transferred power from the White House to the states. Richard was criticized for imposing wage and price controls and, for enforcing desegregation of Southern schools and for setting up the Environmental Protection Agency (EPA).

Lyndon Baines Johnson (1963-1969) was the 36th President. Despite his decision not to run for re-election in 1968, "Johnson's legacy would be forever tarnished by his vast expansion of U.S. involvement in the Vietnam War" (Sarah Pruitt, 2016). Since according to his critics, "The War in Vietnam drove Johnson into depression, and brought his Presidency to an undistinguished end" (Sarah Pruitt, 2016).

John Fitzgerald Kennedy (1961-1963), the 35th President of the United States. He was one of the American Presidents who died through assassination while in power. Though historians tend to rate John Kennedy as a good president aside other Americans who equally consider him as a great one; yet, Kennedy was berated for the covert invasion of Cuba by many liberals such as: Chester Bowles, Arthur Schlesinger, Jr., and John Kenneth Galbraith among others within and outside his own administration (University of Virginia, 2017).

For some politically unclear reasons, Dwight David Eisenhower (1953-1961), the 34th President of the United States' administration was tagged as: crisis government" (CBS NEWs, 2017). Though as one of the post world-war II Presidents, many still hold the opinion that Eisenhower received more positive encomium than negative ratings for his time in office. But despite this unilateral accolade, many writers and scholars have adjudged and criticized his presidency as a lackluster one. In the words of his critics: "He was politically inept and passive. He seemed to hold a minimalist view of the leadership responsibilities of the chief executive" (Fred, 2002).

Harry S. Truman (1945-1953) was the 33rd President of America. He was a statesman and he took over the presidential office upon the death of Franklin Roosevelt. Like his counterparts, he was also accused and criticized for so many things. He was claimed to be the only president in his time who had used veto power more than any president since congress kept blocking most of his unpopular proposals which are mere extension of Franklin Roosevelt's deals. He has also been criticized as the only world leader at his time to have used nuclear weapons in war *(Devine, 2009)*.

Franklin Delano Roosevelt (1933-1945), the 32nd President was acclaimed as "the President who turned America into being Super power" (Greg, 2009). Despite this stance, Roosevelt has been critically and continuously criticized for over-centralization of power to himself. He was said to be in control of the government as well as the Democratic Party. More so, there were worries in the course of his second tenure that he was heading in the direction of dictatorship for his push to seize control of the Supreme Court in 1937-incident called the Court-packing. He also broke the tradition put in place by George Washington when he sought a third term re-election in 1940. In fact, historians wrapped up the event of the time thus: "…with the two-term issue as a weapon, anti-New Dealers... argued that the time had come to disarm the 'dictator' and to dismantle the machinery" (Herbert & Marie, 2013).

Herbert Clark Hoover (1929-1933) was the 31st President of the United States. He was known as a poor communicator. He was accused of fuelling wars and, for exacerbating depression. He was attacked for being too rigid with conservative principles. He was also accused for failing to rise up to the greatest challenges of his time (Tolson, 2017). He was referred to as one of the worse Presidents in American history (Macomber, 2016).

Calvin Coolidge (1923-1929) was the 30th American President. To his credit, he has on record that he was the President who restored public confidence in the White House in their time. But his reputation also went through the eyes of the storm as he was berated for crisis leadership and for failing to work for equal justice for all Americans. He was also accused for failing to use the gains from the economic boom to assist struggling workers and farmers to revamp their businesses (Robert, 1995).

Warren Gamaliel Harding (1921-1923) was the 29th leader of the great America. As a strong politician, he was a popular President. However, some emerging scandals under his administration eroded his popularity in the course of time. Harding's administration was couched by Teapot Dome scandal aside the negative image-problem he incurred on the revelation of his affair with Nan Britton, one of his former mistresses *(Gage, 2008)*.

Woodrow Wilson (1913-1921) was the 28th President. To his credit, he was instrumental towards the establishment of the Paris Peace Conference, same as, Versailles Peace Conference after the World War I. For his initiative and efforts, it was recorded that he won a Nobel Peace Prize. However, Wilson's accusations streamed from his failure to persuade the United States to join this conference. For most journalists of the age, Wilson was only on a mission for self recognition and personal aggrandizement. They believed he was working for self rather than the glory of the United States. According to Los Angeles Times (2018), which quoted Kendrick Clements; a professor of history in South Carolina University: "Wilson (also) failed to stand up for civil rights during and after the war. That failure played a part in the rise of super-patriotism, the persecution of German Americans and war critics, and to a series of deadly race riots in American cities. More than that, it contributed to the rise of anti-immigrant xenophobia after the war, to the revival of the 'Ku Klux Klan' in the 1920s and to a perpetuation of American racism that remains one of our great blots on the national history. It wouldn't have cost him much to have spoken up for tolerance, but he did so only belatedly and timidly. On this matter, he betrayed his own best principles."

William Howard Taft (1909-1913) was the 27th American President. Despite many of his domestic gains during his tenure, William Howard Taft was adjudged to be more of a jury than a politician. He was only President for just one term and according to historian, his tenure was not a pleasant one. The administration was said to be ravaged by conflict between the conservative wing and the progressive wing of the Republican Party. Taft was more of the conservative and he was sympathetic with the group. One of his acute critics was his own mentor, Theodore Roosevelt who also joined others to accuse him of being too liberal. The foreign affair-policies of his government were also criticized. He was widely challenged for his "dollar diplomacy" in East and Latin America. He was also blamed for the diplomatic setbacks his administration suffered when Canada rejected his tariff reciprocity treaty among other issues.

Theodore Roosevelt (1901-1909), the 26th President of America was also said to be successful at the domestic front during his time. However, his fight against corruption got him into severe attacks and persecution by many business owners who tagged him as a socialist. Roosevelt however refuted the accusations and remained unbent in his fight against mal-practices within the system. One of the worse crises of his administration was during the coal strike in 1902. He was in between the sea and high heaven due to the pressure from Republicans and the American citizenry when he threatened to replace the coal workers who were on strike with American troops if a settlement would not be reached to end the strike action. William McKinley (1897-1901), the 25th American President was tagged as an interventionism and a pro-business government. His administration was largely considered to have performed above average. McKinley also earned credits with his successful outing in the war against the Spanish over Cuba conflicts. However, McKinley was accused to be a highly controversial person and, according to historians, the advent of Roosevelt was instrumental to his positive public image down-turn (Hirschfeld, 2015).

President Grover Cleverland (1893-1897) was the only President so far who served two tenures that were not consecutive. He was the 24th and 22nd President of the United States of America. This equally means he won reelection back into office after being defeated as an incumbent. He was largely accused for his attitudinal inconsistence on issue of race. According to historians, "though he spoke out against injustices being perpetuated toward the Chinese in the West, while he agreed with the South's reluctance to treat African Americans as equals socially or politically. And at the same time he felt that Native Americans should be assimilated into white society as quickly as possible, through paternalistic education and land grants. But his policy implementations never reflected his political statements" (History on the Net, 2012). Cleverland was also lambasted for the economic depression of 1893, when about 74 railroads and 600 financial institutions failed.

When the stock market collapsed and lost nearly 35% values. Unemployment statistics for that year was equally as high as 20% with over 15,000 businesses' shut-down among other economic woes that cumulated into his negative public image that cost his failure at the pool when he first bided for reelection after the completion of his first term in office.

Additionally, the three major unfavorable supreme court's rulings at the time equally compounded his public image down-turn woes. Besides the complications he earned through his interference in a boundary dispute between Venezuela and Great Britain, where he threatened war against England. Historians further berated his Presidency as one "with no real vision for the future; nevertheless, Cleverland is at best a preface to the emergence of the modern presidency that began with William McKinley and Theodore Roosevelt." (History on the Net, 2012).

Benjamin Harrison (1889-1893), the 23rd American President was popularly called "little Ben" possibly due to his short stature but many believed that his administration stood tall in relation to foreign policies. But the problems of his presidency were more of domestic issues. He had a tariff problem domestically. His high tariff rate created serious problem for businesses internally. Harrison also failed in the eyes of the public due to his lack of political know-how to public responses. He was equally accused of lack of good rapport with fellow party leaders during his reign.

Chester Alan Arthur (1881-1885) was the 21st President of the United States. To his credit, he rose above partisanship to sign the Pendleton Act of job meritocracy in government.

Arthur however came under serious attacks from the reformers when he was accused of staffing the customs house with party workers rather than officials of the government. He was also berated for his unyielding grounds in major diplomatic matters.

James Abram Garfield (1881) was the 20th President of the United States who died through assassination in September of same year he was sworn into power. He was said to be one of the Presidents with very short time in office, clearly next to William Henry Harrison who died barely one month in office to remain the President with the shortest duration in office in the history of American Presidency till date. Though much could not be written of his presidency due his assassination saga but his brief time in office was marked by political wrangling which might have equally lead to his assassination.

Rutherford Birchard Hayes (1877-1881), the 19th President of America was said to assume office after the reconstruction era. While in office, "he ended Army support for Republican state governments in the South, promoted civil service reform, and attempted to reconcile the divisions left over from the Civil War and Reconstruction" (Loftus, 2016). Although, both the historians and scholars ranked him as an average president, but he has been criticized for ordering the federal troops to take over during the Great Railroad Strike of 1877.

Ulysses S. Grant (1869-1877), the 18th American President was very prominent as an Army General during the American Civil War. To his credit and discredit, it was documented that: "Grant led the Republicans in their effort to remove the vestiges of Confederate nationalism and slavery, protect African-American citizenship and civil rights, implement reconstruction and support economic prosperity. But, Grant's presidency has often been criticized for its scandals and, for his failure to alleviate the economic depression following the Panic of 1873. However, modern scholarship regards him as a president who performed a difficult job during the early post Civil War era" (White, 2016).

Andrew Johnson (1865-1869), the 17th President of the United States was regarded by historians as one of the worse presidents. He also retained the record of the first President of the United States to be impeached by the congress though he was not removed from office. For some political reasons, he was labeled as a traitor. The label may more likely collude with him being fingered in Abraham Lincoln's murder since it was alleged that the murder took place barely six weeks after his inauguration as vice President of the United States in 1865. He was also debased for lacking former education. Historians also claimed that "he turned a blind eye to the southerners who tried to undo what the Civil War had accomplished" (U.S. News, 2014).

Abraham Lincoln (1861-1865) was the 16th President of the United States. Record has it that: "Lincoln led the United States through its Civil War—its bloodiest war and perhaps its greatest moral, constitutional, and political crisis. In doing so, he preserved the Union, paved the way for the abolition of slavery, strengthened the federal government, and modernized the economy" (Louis, 1991). But according to Allen Guelzo, a Professor of history and Civil War-era studies in Gettysburg College: "The worst thing Lincoln did, without question, was pulling the plug on a key Civil War campaign strategy. The clear path for the

Union army to capturing the Confederate capital at Richmond was through the Chesapeake waterways, with the substantial help of the U.S. Navy. But after one of Lincoln's commanding generals, George B. McClellan, botched an early waterborne attempt, and then blamed his failure on Lincoln and began dropping loose rumors about a military coup, Lincoln abruptly reversed course. Even after Lincoln relieved McClellan of his command, any proposal to use the Chesapeake and the Virginia waterways was politically radioactive. For two years after, Union generals and soldiers tried to slog their way overland, along the ladder of Virginia's swamps and rivers, butting into one perfect Confederate defensive position after another and losing thousands of lives in the process. Lincoln was a skilled political thinker but a military amateur, dealing with ideas of strategy that he extracted from out-of-date military manuals" (Los Angeles Times, 2018).

James Buchanan (1857-1861) was the 15th President of the United States who was often referred to as "doughface" for being a Northern with Southern sympathies. According to Tolson, (2007) however, Buchanan's accusations included the allegation that he refused to challenge the spread of slavery. He also refused to challenge the growth among the states that became the confederacy. "More damaging to his name, though, was his weak acquiescence before the secessionist tide—an unwillingness to challenge those states that declared their intention to withdraw from the Union after Lincoln's election. Sitting on his hands as the situation spiraled out of control; Buchanan believed that the Constitution gave him no power to act against would-be secessionists" (Tolson, 2007).

Franklin Pierce (1853-1857) was the 14th President of the United States. Pierce's name surfaces on the list of worse presidents of America as compiled by the historians. According to Larry Gara, the Author of "The Presidency of Franklin Pierce," "The best thing Pierce did as president had to do with excrement. Specifically, guano, or bird droppings, which were so essential to U.S. agriculture in the mid-1800s that the era is sometimes referred to as the Golden Age of Guano" (Los Angeles Times, 2018). But beyond this, he was largely critic as a "Mexican War veteran who believed ardently in national expansion even at the cost of adding more slave states" (Tolson, 2007). According to Tolson (2007), Theodore Roosevelt painted him as "a servile tool of men worse than himself ... ever ready to do any work the slavery leaders set him."

Millard Fillmore (1850-1853) was the 13th President of the United States. He benefitted from the demise of Zachary Taylor, the popular war hero who died in office. This was the reason Miller became the 13th President of the United States. He was however among the President classified by historians as worse Presidents of the United States. His own accusations stemmed from backing the compromise that took place in 1850. This compromise delayed the secession of the Southerners, which cumulated into the spread of slavery.

Zachary Taylor (1849-1850) was the 12th President of the United States. Zachary was a war hero who died in office barely one year into his first tenure. He was classified as a forgettable President who was worse more than a failed one. According to his critics, he was a politically attuned man and as such, least expected to have occupied the White House. According to historians, he was "a slaveholder who defended the "peculiar institution" in the South, he opposed its extension into new states as vigorously as he objected to the idea of secession" (Tolson, 2007).

James Knox Polk (1845-1849) was the 11th President of the United States of America. Pork was largely recognized and appraised for his faithfulness to keeping his campaign promises. It was recorded that he met every major domestic and foreign policies he set as promises during his political campaign. However, his critics came up with strong accusation of his misconduct that: "he misrepresented strength of abolitionism, grossly exaggerated likelihood of slaves' massacring white families and seemed to condone secession" (Dusinberre, 2002).

John Tyler (1841-1845) was the 10th President of the United States of America. He was a president who served the major part of his term without party affiliation since he broke from the Whig agenda, and was expelled from his party. Tyler came into power by succeeding his incumbent, William Harrison who died in office barely one month after his inauguration. Tyler was known to be a strong defender of the slavery system (Crapol, 2006). According to Edward P. Crapol, History professor emeritus of the College of William and Mary *"Tyler is one of just two U.S. presidents to serve part of his term without party affiliation, and his ineffectiveness in office has been attributed in part to his isolation from the political process. One newspaper editor, who was also a leader of the Whig party, called Tyler a "poor, miserable, despised imbecile." (Los Angeles Time, 2018).*

William Henry Harrison (1841) was the 9th President of the United States of America who lasted for just one month in office before his demise (*Gasaway, 1999*). According to Tolson (2007), "that the ninth president makes any list at all is an act of scholarly injustice, since he was president for just 30 days after contracting pneumonia during his interminable and, he was actually fore-warned the death became imminent."

Martin Van Buren (1837-1841) was the 8th President of the United States. According to historians, he was once among the America's most famous politicians. He ranked first in history on certain policies such as "the first president to address the national government's powers to tackle a national economic crisis" (*Lacroix, 2016*). However, he soon became hated for his active roles to perpetrate slavery. His political popularity was further wrecked when "the first great depression happened on his watch; couple with his conviction that the federal government lacked the authority to do much in response to the crisis. This wrecked his presidency and it became an example for subsequent presidents to avoid" He was also criticized for "denying the application of Texas for admission to the Union, concerned that it would undermine the North-South balance in Congress and touch off an acrimonious debate over the extension of slavery, as happened in 1819 over Missouri statehood, and hoping to avoid war with Mexico" (*Lacroix, 2016*).

Andrew Jackson (1829-1837) was the 7th President of the United States of America. He was highly appraised for seeking to act as "the direct representative of the common man," having being elected by popular vote. His accusers among whom are Henry Clay, Daniel Webster, and other Whig leaders stated "the fact that Jackson, unlike previous Presidents, did not defer to Congress in policy-making but used his power of the veto and his party leadership to assume command. His violence approach to opposition was also decried when South Carolina undertook to nullify the tariff, Jackson ordered armed forces to Charleston and privately threatened to hang Calhoun.

Violence seemed imminent until Clay negotiated a compromise: tariffs were lowered and South Carolina dropped nullification. As also in January of 1832, while the President was dining with friends at the White House, someone whispered to him that the Senate had rejected the nomination of Martin Van Buren as Minister to England. Jackson jumped to his feet and exclaimed, "By the Eternal! I'll smash them!" So he did. His favorite, Van Buren, became Vice President, and succeeded to the Presidency when "Old Hickory" retired to the Hermitage, where he died in June 1845" (Frank and Hugh, 2006). He was the first president however to have an assassination-attempt attack on him while in office.

John Quincy Adams (1825-1829) was the 6th President of the United States. His effort and initiative to come up with a policy to modernize the economy of the United States was well appraised. However, "his popularity declined as a result of his lenient approach toward Native Americans, whom he supported against the demands of westward settlers" He was also crucified for the protective tariff that was popularly tagged as "Tariff of Abominations" during his reign. His oppositions also found him to be pursuing ambitious domestic agenda when "he envisioned a national marketplace in which North and South, town and country, would be tied together by trade and exchange" (*Ede, 2014*).

James Monroe (1817-1825) was the 5th President of the United States of America. He was a President well commended for his talented international relation according to historians. He was credit with the establishment of the Monroe Doctrine which severed European nations from colonizing or interfering with Western Hemisphere. Despite his many honors however, modern historians have criticized him vigorously because "His administration supported the founding of colonies in Africa for freed slaves that eventually form the bulk of business activities for the western world in his century" (*James, 2017*).

James Madison (1809-1817) was the 4th President of the United States of America. He was one of the major leaders of his era to ratify and implement the newly drafted constitution of the United States. He came up with lots of bills and policies to promote trade and improve the economy of America while alienating many European countries against the United Kingdom in his time. However, he was critically accused of self-contradiction after accepting to pursue the creation of national bank, which he had long opposed. Madison was also accused by modern historians as "a slaveholder who inherited his plantation known as Montpelier, and owned hundreds of slaves during his life time to cultivate tobacco and other crops. He was also berated for his support for the Three-Fifths Compromise that allowed three-fifths of the enumerated population of slaves to be counted for representation" (Hawks, 2012).

Thomas Jefferson (1801-1809) was the 3rd President of the United States of America. Jefferson was one of the founding fathers of America and his critical role has been recognized as the principal person behind the declaration of independence. Historians scripted that he "motivated American colonists to break from Great Britain and form a new nation, he produced formative documents and nation building decisions at both the state and national level" (*Brewer, 1997). However, he was seriously accused of* throwing the US economy into what was described as untold suffering when he banned foreign trade to coerce a resolution which he never achieved until he lifted the ban before he left office during his second term. Jefferson was further criticized as a critical and a very complicated person. In fact in the words of Andrew Burstein, a Professor of history in Louisiana State University: "Perhaps the worst thing Jefferson did as president was to prosecute first and ask questions later. He arranged for the impeachment of an associate justice of the Supreme Court who was really only guilty of having a big mouth. That failed. Later, he publicly accused his first-term vice president, Aaron Burr, of committing treason. In this instance, Jefferson chose to believe the word of a corrupt general and wild rumor printed in biased newspapers. I have never quite figured out why Jefferson only became chummy with Burr after Burr shot and killed Alexander Hamilton"(Los Angeles Times, 2018).

John Adams (1797-1801) was the 2nd President to occupy the White House of the United States of America. He ran a war-dominated term of office. According to historians, "His tenure as president was dominated by the Quasi-War, an undeclared war against the French Republic waged primarily in the Caribbean. The conflict grew out of the so-called XYZ Affair, a political and diplomatic episode during the first year of Adams administration, and had its roots in the turbulent state of Franco–American relations following the 1789 French Revolution. In 1798, as the toll from attacks on American shipping and the possibility of war with France increased, Adams directed an expansion of the U.S. Navy, and creation of the Department of the Navy to manage it. The increased expenditures associated with these actions required greater federal revenue, and Congress passed the Direct Tax of 1798. The war and its associated taxation provoked domestic unrest, resulting in incidents such as Fries's Rebellion." His criticism deepened when he signed into law "the 5th Congress' passed four bills, which were collectively known as the Alien and Sedition Acts. The acts which made it more difficult for immigrants to become U.S. citizens. The act which also allowed the president to imprison and deport non-citizens who were deemed dangerous or who were from a hostile nation, and criminalized making false statements that were critical of the federal government" *(Wood,2009)*.

George Washington (1789-1797) was the first President of the United States. He was the first man to occupy the White House. He was unanimously elected into office in both the first and his second term of office. According to historians, "he had established his preeminence among the new nation's Founding Fathers through his service as Commander-in-Chief of the Continental Army during the American Revolutionary War and as president of the 1787 Constitutional Convention. Once the Constitution was approved, it was widely expected that Washington would become the first President of the United States, despite his own desire to retire from public life. In his first inaugural address, Washington expressed both his reluctance to accept the presidency and his inexperience with the duties of civil administration, but he proved an able leader" He was the only President who never got affiliated with a political party due to his concerns for holding the nation together in Unity rather than encouraging rivalry at that nascent stage of the nation's independence and democracy. "In spite of his efforts, debates over Hamilton's economic policy, the French Revolution, and the Jay Treaty deepened ideological divisions. Those that supported Hamilton formed the Federalist Party, while his opponents coalesced around Secretary of State Thomas Jefferson and formed the Democratic-Republican Party. While criticized for furthering the partisanship he sought to avoid by identifying himself with Hamilton, Washington is nonetheless considered by scholars and political historians as one of the greatest presidents in American history, usually ranking in the top three with Abraham Lincoln and Franklin Delano Roosevelt." (*Solomont, 2015*). Till date, George Washington remained the only President that has not been some-worth criticized and historians held this to his non-partisanship approach to leadership. *Solomont (2015) captured this belief better when he explained the legacy of George Washington himself thus:* "His farewell address reflected this suffering when he warned his fellow citizens 'against the baneful effects' of the party spirit. It 'agitates the community with ill-founded jealousies and false alarms,' creates animosities, and foments "riots and insurrection."

It may sound rough however, reading through the different accusations and media-political challenges that had confronted most of the past presidents of the United States from the review-recaps above. Nevertheless, comparing such individual past experiences to the reality of President Donald Trump's experience today will be as mere introduction to what Trump has been through in his little time in office. President Donald J. Trump has been through a whole lot of tough, rugged, mesmerizing, confrontational, image-degrading, personality-rubbishing and attack-prone situations from the process of his political campaign to his early days in office. These have been his experience right from the moment he began to append his signatures to his presidential policy-directives or executive orders within the very first year of his tenure. In my opinion, I may not be wrong to assert that the most persecuted, rejected, labeled, bombarded, castigated, insulted and hated President that has ever reined on the America's home soil is President Donald J. Trump. The current President has been hated for known and unknown issues. News media had interviewed people who hate him because members of their racial group hate him. There have been people who hate him because he was not their popular choice. Some had felt he was not politically fanciful for America presidency. His hatred has equally streamed from the known issues of politics and policies to the inexplicable news-reports around his personality. Some had disliked him as an over-meticulous business man; others disdained him as a man with many failed marriages. Some claimed it is due to his vulgar language; while others asserted he engaged in tax-fraud. Many other nationals within and outside the United States have equally added their opinions by claiming he does not deserve to be the President. In fact, some trained their pets to exhibit repulsive mannerism at the sight of him on television or other social platforms. Just as some leaders around the world have refused to recognize with his nonpoliticking approach to issues and, they must have equally disliked him for his outspoken style of leadership. And, may be, for his twitter-handle politics. In fact, the list is long. But the greatest battle of representation seems to lie with the media who are in the battle of negative image projection with the greatest office that weigh the most power on the planet earth. Whatever the pattern of the dislike may be or has been however, the 45th President of America, Mr. Donald J. Trump has consistently passed a body language that indicates he is indifferent and, to be candid, the president seems to be "a-one-man army" who is less careful about throng-confrontation along the path of his policies and political movement. On issues of threats or insults, few men exist among whom today has revealed President Donald Trump to be one, who is never perturbed by negative confrontations or reactions. From his process of political campaign to the point of swearing in and policy making, I believe, there is nothing more to prove to Trump's oppositions that the man cannot be couched by protests or threats of unpleasant reportage about his personality and activities. Nevertheless, it is believed that a man cannot be treated in isolation of his history and antecedents. This informs the need to attempt a brief narrative of his personal, family, business-history, media-involvement, political life and campaign processes, up to the point of his emergence as the 45th President of the United States of America. This review-centered book can only surge forward and smoothly when a vivid background narrative has been accomplished on President Donald J. Trump.

CHAPTER THREE

3.0 INTRODUCTION TO THE POLITICS, ECONOMIC HISTORY AND FAMILY LIFE OF THE 45TH PRESIDENT OF AMERICA

3.1   Who Is Donald Trump?

Donald Trump can be best described as the smart 71 years old man who took his time to launch and re-launch himself into the world of relevance during his own generation. He moved from his dominance of one sector to another. As a business mogul, he was a force to be reckoned and respected in the league of successful business men. As a media icon, he got introduced into the sector and ruled the stage while it last. As a politician, Trump understood quiet well that politic is a product and he prepared himself to market it. He studied the situation of his time and flew with the right proposal for his waiting audience. He stresslessly vied for the highest position possible in the realm; campaigned against the prominent politicians of his time and indeed, against the world. Trump mysteriously won against the popular interest of the Sooth-Sayers. Who then is Donald J. Trump? He is an intriguing man. With him, there is no dull moment. Historians may soon concur he has been the most entertaining President of all ages. Not even the Washington D.C.'s White Castle could take his tweeter-handle away from his palm-press.

Donald was in business to make money. He went into the media to make fame. He got into politics to win power. Howbeit, whichever sector he turned, Donald was usually at the top of the game. It has been hard to beat him to his game. It should not be hard to accord honor to whom honor is due. To give respect to whom occasion says it is worth it.

Millions of men have toiled for years to make hay in business to no avail. A thousand others have attempted to gain popularity through the media yet unsuccessful. While decades-long politicians have eyed the seat of American power-house to be the number one man in the world, yet, their formulae never produced results. Who then is Donald J. Trump? How did he gain power? What was his strategy, his procedure or policy-guide to gaining the number one position in the leading nation of the world? To say the truth, Donald is currently one of the living-legends who have tasted the two most critical levels of elitist in the history of human existence. The world has not produced many economic elites like Donald who were able to transform their wealth into political power. Since the political sector has always been dictated by some clique of super-men called the king-makers. Where it becomes imperative to be loyal to the king makers if you must taste from the pot of power. But somehow, Donald the former economic elite filed up against the establishment. He challenged them all in his near-political-party-less campaigns, since the major sections of the party itself disowned him at that critical period of campaigns. But somehow, either by Russia influence or by Electoral College as it has been popularly alleged; historians have only included a name on the cabinet of America's presidency and, that name is: Donald J. Trump, the 45th President of the United States. He was the political shock of 2016.

3.2   Donald J. Trump's 'MFP' Approach to Power

Money: Donald started out his career in life as a business man, building wealth. Since many realities of life have confirmed the statement in the holy book which posits that: "Money answereth all things." Hence, Donald prioritized gaining wealth through his business adventures and he succeeded as one of the billionaires the world has produced as at today.

Fame: Donald took his time to understand the tempo of his generation. Like the popular adage goes, if you can't beat them, you can join them. He recognized that one of the channels of fame-gaining and self-establishment into the social centre is through the media, thus, he went for it. Donald packaged and re-packaged show-biz programs called reality shows until he became a house-hold name through the power of the media. Hence, the smart 71 years old man became a media personality, throwing up all sorts of noise generating and people-enchanting activities until he hit the mark of reckoning. Of course, Donald enhanced his reach through the first commodity he built, which was wealth, to finance his projects. The smart elderly man had a sequence of progression. He was definitely not a fool to place the first priority last or the last priority first. Like the popular adage, he knew the logic of using money to make money. Better still, he understood the principle of using what you have to achieve what you need. He used his wealth to reach for fame. Hence, Donald built FAME after gaining MONEY. But having realized money alone was not enough to get him to achieve his ultimate dream; he was willing to part with some through self-sponsored media programs. No doubt, not every wealthy individual today are famous. Most of them only get mentioned periodically through Forbes or through their annual financial records. Most billionaires around the world cannot even be recognized facially. So Donald didn't want to be recognized just by mere financial documents. His behavior showed he wanted it all. He didn't want to live in the past while he still lives on the planet earth. He wanted to remain in the news. He wanted to create his own face-value. He wanted to be seen. He wanted to be heard just the way millions of people follow after media-faces even though the entertainers over whom they are passionate may have no meaningful financial reserves in their bank accounts. He obviously wanted a name beyond his financial statements and, the media remains the only tool through which that name can be in-scripted in the minds of the common citizens.

Donald wasn't a father-Christmas when he dole-out money and gift items to enhance his entertainment packages. Rather, he was a smart business man on a mission to sell his name at the cost of his money. Also, as a build up to coast towards his carefully arranged career into the American presidency. One more principle to learn from his strategies; Donald was not agitated, rather, he was consistent and he patiently built his media profile through time. He recognized the best period to play the second fiddle through the blame-game approach, which he traded with Barrack Obama's Administration. Many light-thinkers might have thought the man disliked Barack Obama so bad. But no, all the blame games were part of his publicity-package. If you want to beat the king, you simply have to play it out with the king. You don't target the throne and engage the market. There may remain nothing personal between Barrack Obama and Donald J. Trump outside their individual push for self interest. Additionally, the smart Donald knew the right time to unfold and launch his career. This connotes that he observed seasons and understood timing. He may likely possess the potentials to read the stars (I am yet to explore that aspect of him anyway) because Donald J. Trump recognized the criticality of the Obama movement in Obama's time so he didn't interrupt it by being too hurry to run. The smart business man knew it was impossible to run against a man whose time has come so he didn't attempt it until his own season emerged. Little wonder why the smart elderly man smiled against the world while the drums were beating so hard as if he was out of the race to Presidency until he shocked the minds that taunted and berated him. It was very hard to see a politician like him, who was so confident he was going to win even amidst visible hatred.

Product: Donald built product. He didn't build campaign arguments. Rather, he built socio-political product. Donald studied the unvoiced intentions and the body-language of a section of the society and launched a political movement or campaign-product in this direction. The product he brought to the table already had an existing market. In his own campaign, this was what many people found so difficult to understand; because Donald wasn't trying to educate or orient his electorate-market about what he would like to do. Rather, his campaign was to build the confidence of his electorates in him that he can actually do what they wanted him to do. Howbeit, some folks will never understand Donald was not the principal idealist of "Build the Wall campaign." Howbeit, many folks will not understand Donald was not the inventor of "Muslim Influx must stop." Howbeit, some folks will not understand that illegal immigrants are pluses to business owners (or the capitalists) among whom Donald is one. Hence, Donald as a smart business man who understands the input cost ratio may not have been in the fore front of the campaign about illegal immigrant must-go, judging him differently as a business man that he is. But somehow, repatriation is one of his market-product deals with his electorates. In other words, that is what his political market demanded. And, as a fundamental business man, only higher forces may prevail against him not to satisfy his market, since that is what business owners are known for: market satisfaction.

3.3   The Family Life of Donald John Trump

Reference his lineage, Donald John Trump was born by a Lutheran father (Fred Trump) who hailed from Germany while his Presbyterian mother (Mary Anne MacLeod Trump) hailed from Scotland. Donald himself was born on the 14th of June, 1946 as the fourth child of five children. His siblings included: Fred Trump Jr., Robert Trump, Maryanne Trump Barry and Elizabeth Trump Grau. Donald Trump grew up in Borough of Queens, New York City. He attended Kew-Forest School. He was enrolled in the New York Military Academy from 1964. He went to Fordham University from 1964 to 1966. While he eventually attained a degree in Economics from Wharton School of the University of Pennsylvania in 1968 (*Panetta, 2015*).

Donald married Ivana his first wife and the marriage lasted for fifteen years (1977 to 1992). Ivana Trump is a Czech American business woman and she was a fashion model. Donald and Ivana had three children together. These included: Donald Trump Jr., (39 years old); Ivanka Trump (35 years old) and Eric Trump (33 years old) (Osmanski, 2017). Donald J. Trump married his second wife named Marla Maples in 1993. Marla was an American actress and television personality. The marriage ended in 1999. Both Marla and Donald however had a twenty-four (24) years old daughter together called: Tiffany Trump. Finally, Donald Trump married his current wife and first lady, Melania Trump in the year 2005 and the marriage has produced an eleven (11) years old son named: Baron Trump.

As a sport lover, he has been known with soccer, wrestling, football, baseball and, his current sport seems to be Gulf. Most obviously, Donald is a man who wants to have a feel of everything happening in the world around him.

3.4   Donald Trump's Brief Business-History

According to *Stump (2016) "Trump* followed in the footsteps of his grandmother Elizabeth and father Fred in running the family's real estate company, which he renamed The Trump Organization. He managed the business from 1971 until his 2017 inauguration as president. Trump's real estate career focused on building or renovating skyscrapers, hotels, casinos, and golf courses. He also started multiple side ventures, branded and licensed his name for real estate and various products. Stump (2015) further by quoting President Trump himself, when he said: "he began his career with 'a small loan of one million dollars' from his father. But as at the time of his appearance on the initial Forbes 400 list of wealthy individuals in 1982, Donald surfaced with an estimated $200 million fortune, including an "undefined" share of his parents' estate. In fact, as of late 1980s, Donald was already a billionaire and he made the Forbes World's Billionaires list for the first time in 1989. Although his business experienced some turbulence between 1990 and 1995 but he soon shore up."

Rozhon (2017) captured Donald Trump's Manhattan development and business deal with this specificity: "In 1978, Trump launched his Manhattan real estate business by purchasing a 50% stake in the financially troubled Commodore Hotel. The purchase was largely funded by a $70 million construction loan that was jointly guaranteed by Fred Trump and the Hyatt hotel chain. When the remodeling was finished, the hotel reopened as the Grand Hyatt Hotel, located next to Grand Central Terminal. Also in the same 1978, Trump finished negotiations to develop Trump Tower, a 58-story, 202-meter (663-foot) skyscraper in Midtown Manhattan, which The New York Times attributed to his "persistence" and "skills as a negotiator". The building was eventually completed in 1983 and houses both the primary penthouse condominium residence of Trump and the headquarters of The Trump Organization. In 1985, Trump acquired the Mar-a-Lago estate in Palm Beach, Florida for under $8 million. The home was built in the 1920s by heiress and socialite Marjorie Merriweather Post, who envisioned the house as a future winter retreat for American presidents. In 1986, Trump acquired a foreclosed 33-story, twin-tower condominium complex in nearby West Palm Beach for $40 million.

Auto CEO Lee Iacocca invested in three of the condos. Trump spruced up the complex's public areas and heavily promoted the property for years, but selling the units proved difficult, and the deal turned out to be unprofitable. He also soaked that up in the course of time."

Razhon (2017) furthered that "In 1988 Trump acquired the Plaza Hotel in Manhattan for a record-setting $407 million and appointed his wife Ivana to manage its operation. Trump invested $50 million to restore the building, which he called "the Mona Lisa." According to hotel expert Thomas McConnell, the Trumps boosted it from a three-star to a four-star ranking and sold it in 1995, by which time Ivana was no longer involved in the hotel's day-to-day operations. In 1994, Trump got involved with the refurbishing of the Gulf and Western Building on Columbus Circle. The former office building was remodeled with design and structural enhancements to become a luxury residential and hotel property. When the job was finished, Trump owned commercial space is a 44-story tower (hotel and condominium) that he named Trump International Hotel and Tower. In 1996, Trump acquired the Bank of Manhattan Trust Building, which was a vacant seventy-one story skyscraper on Wall Street that had briefly been the tallest building in the world when it was completed in 1930. After an extensive renovation, the high-rise was renamed the Trump Building at 40 Wall Street. In 1997, he began construction on Riverside South, which he dubbed Trump Place, a multi-building development along the Hudson River. The project encountered delays the following year because a subcontractor had to replace defective concrete and due to this, he and the other investors in the project ultimately sold their interest for $1.8 billion in 2005 in what was then the biggest residential sale in the history of New York City."

"From 1994 to 2002, Trump owned a 50% share of the Empire State Building. He would have renamed it "Trump Empire State Building Tower Apartments" if he had been able to boost his share, it was believed. In 2001, Trump completed Trump World Tower, which was across from the headquarters of the United Nations. For a while, the structure was the tallest all-residential tower in the world. In 2002, Trump acquired the former Hotel Delmonico, which was renovated and reopened in 2004 as the Trump Park Avenue; the building consisted of 35 stories of luxury condominiums. Meanwhile, he continued to own millions of square feet of other prime Manhattan real estate as time passes. In 2006, Trump bought 1,400 acres (570 ha), including the Menie Estate in Balmedie, Aberdeenshire, Scotland, and created a golf resort there. Scottish supporters emphasized potential economic benefits, and opponents emphasized potential environmental harm to a Site of Special Scientific Interest. (SSSI). A spokesperson for the golf course has said 95% of the SSSI is untouched. A 2011 independent documentary, You've Been Trumped, chronicled the golf resort's construction and struggles. In 2015, an offshore windfarm being built within sight of the golf course prompted a legal challenge by Trump, which was dismissed by the U.K. Supreme Court. In the wake of the 2008 recession, Trump greatly scaled back development of this property, and as of December 2016 Scottish officials were pushing for completion of the far larger development as originally approved. In April 2014, Trump purchased the Turnberry hotel and golf resort in Ayrshire, Scotland, which hosted the Open Championship four times between 1977 and 2009. After extensive renovations and a remodeling of the course by golf architect Martin Ebert, Turnberry was reopened in June 2016" (Razhon, 2017).

The above is a mere attempt to capture the expansive business exploit of the man currently holding the office of the socio-economic and political life of America. If the list of his private achievement is real as documented by many news editors, historians and scholars, it may worth the trial to accord him the space to expand the fortune of America since by virtue of providence, he is already the president.

3.5   Donald Trump's Media-Involvement

Donald Trump walked his ways into the heart of the fourth estate of the realm called Media with his television reality shows. According to Stump *(2016)*, *"Trump* gained prominence in the media and entertainment fields. He co authored several books (most notably *The Art of the Deal*), and from 2003 to 2015 he was a producer and the host of *The Apprentice*, a reality television game show. Trump also owned the Miss Universe and Miss USA beauty pageants from 1996 to 2015.

Rozhon, (2017) equally touched on Donald's involvement with pageant programs around the world when she wrote "From 1996 to 2015, Trump owned part or all of the Miss Universe pageants. The Miss Universe pageants include Miss USA and Miss Teen USA, and his management of this business involved his family members, especially Ivanka."

3.6   Donald Trump and His Historic Political Debut

Based on records, Donald Trump had interacted with politics in the past through several peripheral involvements as a critic, opinionist and/or as a financial or campaign donor. But he had never run as a candidate for any political office previously. In this regard, Donald Trump was a freshman coming into the political landslide to give a shot at the presidential office. Hence, he was never a politician until 2015 when he declared his intentions and went for nomination. According to Rozhon (2017)."Trump announced his candidacy for the presidency on June 16, 2015. Subsequently, he entered the 2016 race as a Republican and significantly defeated sixteen opponents in the primaries. Commentators described his political positions as populist, protectionist, and nationalist. His campaign received extensive free media coverage due to his categorical public statements, which many considered as controversial. Trump won the 2016 general election against Democratic opponent Hillary Clinton. He became the oldest and wealthiest person ever to assume the presidency, the first without prior military or government service, and the fifth to have won the election despite losing the popular vote. However, his election and policies have since been sparking numerous protests."

Nevertheless, to the common American historians, this man called Donald Trump does not have the historical pattern or standardization that suits the position of America President but this is where the sharp disagreement comes to the fore, once again, between those who uphold the virtue of "God's Existence," who feel that the God's unseen ruling-hand is in the affairs of men; as against those who says there is no God. Those who simply believe everything in life is achievable through some procedural processes or natural principles alone. The spiritual versus the naturalist. No doubt, on assumption of office, the emerging 45th President of America quickly declared the side he belongs. How worried am I as a student of spiritualism therefore? I am afraid the history behind such installations maintains that 'those who are installed by the forces beyond human capacity, human understanding, human interest or opinion' can never be moved. I may not need a counter opinion to convince me otherwise on the basis of debates; I will only look forward to see the reality of this spiritual verdict changed before I can be convinced that the unseen being called: God, does not rule in the affairs of men; my take.

CHAPTER FOUR

4.0 DONALD TRUMP AND THE CONCEPT OF INVISIBLE POLITICS

The concept of invisible politics demonstrates a deviation from the norm. In statistical perception, deviation from the norm is recognized as: "the difference between an observed value of a variable and its mean. This is also called the mean deviation from the mean (or median), average deviation is a measure of dispersion derived by computing the mean of the absolute values of the differences between observed values of a variable and the variable's mean." In lay man's language: "Deviation means doing something that is different from what people consider to be normal or acceptable, which is often not tolerated due to human's attitude to change" Webster (2010). In other words, invisible politics can be described as Donald Trump's concept of governance. This concept is his business approach or pattern to governance as against the traditional pattern of politicking called political lobbying. Of a truth, most interests of the common man have been largely jeopardized through what politicians referred to as lobbying, which is simply a way of "giving and taking amongst themselves (the politicians)."

In nations of Africa for instance, where political lobbying has played a dangerous role in corruption enhancement. The legislative arm in most of those countries trade (law-making) votes for approval of personal projects or money lodgments into their personal accounts by the executive arm. This has largely wrecked most of these third world economies where so many state resources have been lobbied into private pockets.

The reigning president of the United States of America has been a business man all his life. Credit to destiny he won the seat of power in his (first) debut into politics. The transition from the position of the chief executive officer/president of a business oriented Private Corporation to the position of the commander in chief and president in charge of the economy of a nation without special school on political or politicking-orientation can only dictate one thing. This singular thing is the business approach to the issues of governance. To some sound thinkers and students of change, this may be a good deal as a deviation from the norm. But, definitely, those who have lived for too long with the politicking approach to governance may never be able to find the new pattern of governance easy or acceptable. May be, not so soon. Hence, rather than politicking with his policy-strategies for legislative approval, Donald Trump negotiates from the business-front. He employed the principles of "relevancy to project" and "mission consistency" to keep his government in focus despite the decision or indecision of other factors.

In Trump's statements on issues bothering on bilateral or multilateral relations with other nations of the world, he inscribed it boldly that it is no longer business as usual. America may no longer be father-Christmas since indeed; there is no free gift in international politics. On the fight against terrorism, it was written, it can no longer be tendered with gloves hands. Politicians can no longer be sitting and just talk or argue when precious and innocent lives are being killed for nothing on the daily basis. It is the dawn of business approach to governance, it seems.

Since, in business, you reap just exactly what you sow. If you sow terror, you get terror in higher magnitude. Without doubt, Syria was the first to taste from this business-promise of President Donald J. Trump. In the words of Tom (2017) "U.S. Navy guided-missile destroyer USS Porter (DDG 78) conducts strike operations while in the Mediterranean Sea, which U.S. Defense Department said was a part of cruise missile strike against Syria on April 7, 2017. The attack came less than 72 hours after the U.S. accused Syrian President Bashar al-Assad of ordering a chemical weapons attack against civilians and marked a major divergence in policy between former political allies, President Donald Trump and his Russian counterpart, President Vladimir Putin."

The term invisibility does not however mean non-existence. This means Trump still tries to engage in political negotiations but in a more business-like. Since, invisibility only implies: unnoticeable, useable, intangible, inconspicuous and insignificant. According to Oxfords dictionary, invisibility means inability to be seen. Wikipedia gives invisibility more broader analysis, stating that: "Invisibility is the state of an object that cannot be seen. An object in this state is said to be invisible (literally, "not visible"). The term is often used in fantasy/science fiction, where objects cannot be seen by magical or technological means; however, its effects can also be demonstrated in the real world, particularly in physics and perceptual psychology classes. Since objects can be seen by light in the visible spectrum from a source reflecting off their surfaces and hitting the viewer's eye, the most natural form of invisibility (whether real or fictional) is an object that neither reflects nor absorbs light (that is, it allows light to pass through it). This is known as transparency, and is seen in many naturally occurring materials (although no naturally occurring material is 100% transparent). Invisibility perception depends on several optical and visual factors. For example, invisibility depends on the eyes of the observer and/or the instruments used. Thus an object can be classified as "invisible to" a person, animal, instrument, etc. In research on sensorial perception it has been shown that invisibility is perceived in cycles. Invisibility is also often considered to be the supreme form of camouflage, as it does not reveal to the viewer any kind of vital signs, visual effects, or any frequencies of the electromagnetic spectrum detectable to the human eye, instead making use of radio, infrared or ultraviolet wavelengths. In illusion optics, invisibility is a special case of illusion effects: the illusion of free space." Whatever the description and applicability of invisibility may be however, the reality of the new generation and pattern of Donald Trump's approach to governance has reduced the traditional practice of politicking and lobbying and, has substantially replaced it with business-like approach to governance.

CHAPTER FIVE

5.0 AMERICA'S IMMIGRATION POLICY UNDER DONALD TRUMP: MY TAKE!!!

Sometimes, it is okay to be emotional. Every living being has that potency. But those who have made it through life, and succeeded, are actually the realists. Nonetheless, there is a place for emotion and there is a time to face reality.

To start with, sometime it is worth to enhance understanding through story-telling. This therefore occasioned the need for this story analogy to drive more understanding around the wisdom behind critical immigration policies some nations of the world have had to embark upon at certain time in their history. Sometimes, things are never meant to be the same since the only thing constant in life is change itself: "With keen interest, there was a scene of robbery that beckoned attention. There was an armed robber arrested in a local community. The fate on this armed robber suddenly lied in the hands of the assailants who were trying to lynch him. Some community members started feeling sorry for the armed robber after a period of torture by the youth and, more so, when the armed robber started begging them for his own life. But unfortunately for the armed robber, just as the sympathizers almost coercing the aggressive youths to rescind their interest lynching him, news broke from the neighboring town that the same armed robber had operated in two compounds about 2 days before he now met his waterloo in the next operation. In the course of his last operation in those compounds he previously invaded; it was reported, he did terrible and unimaginable things including: (i) wiping out an entire family of four; father, mother and two kids after sleeping with their two (2) daughters because the man, whose house he burgled, couldn't offer him whatever he must have demanded of him; (ii) this same armed robber made two siblings of the same parents to commit incest because he forced those kids to sleep with each other at gun point while he watched the siblings with fun; (iii) he also killed a gate man and the street guard on the same day. But here is the same robber now begging and heaping up emotions for people to have pity on him to preserve his own life, since he has now been caught."

This scenario helps to give some coloration to the situation of visa suspension in some religiously fanatical nations trooping into the United States. Like the saying goes; 'he whose mother was killed by a mad man will be wary of a tattered-looking wanderer when he sees one.' It is not also good to experience some measure of chaos before learning vital lessons from such. Many countries in Africa and Middle East that have been devastated by internal chaos due to the population of religious fanatics it harbors will understand these lines of advice better. Without doubt, it takes experience to know that any time some of these religious fanatics have the chance to hit and kill others, they don't mix emotions with it, but when they need what you have which could make them to harvest the result of their decades of outright rejection and killing of others in the name of belief, they reach for people's emotions to push for their needs especially from the good loving American Christians.

America's situation has also been likened to that of a hunter who went hunting and, in the course of time, he found a cute-looking cub (a small lion) lonely in the bush. He felt so compassionate that he took the cub with him into his own household. The hunter went to the extent of depriving his own kids certain benefits to be able to give life to this cute cub. However, in the course of time, the cub grew into a giant Lion and unfortunately, the hunter forgot one day to make adequate provisions on ground before embarking on a journey that lasted one-straight week. After the third day of his departure, the lion ran out of his daily provisions. By the fifth day, it grew so hungry and veracious. By the morning of the sixth day, the ravenous-looking lion descended on the two promising kids this hunter had in this world and fed on them. This was how the great hunter innocently destroyed himself. This lion-story has been a historic proverb told by the generations before this age to caution the younger generation about future consequences of every action taken today which may look so innocent and harmless for the moment.

Like the warning statement echoes; 'you don't use your own hands to bring troubles onto your own household while trying to help others.' It has equally been said that people usually lock their doors every night, not because they hate their neighbors but because they care more about the safety of their children and the valuables they have behind those doors.

Donald Trumps' immigration policies have revolves more around: Executive Order or Visa bans to DACA and, to repatriation of illegal aliens. These policy-orders shall be reviewed one after the other in the subsequent sub-topics.

5.1   Trump's Executive Order Or Visa Ban & The Historical Background To It

From time immemorial, nations of the world have been coming up with immigration laws to restrict other nationals into their territories especially due to perceived insecurity of any kind. President Chester Alan Arthur (1881-1885), the 21st American President was the first to ban other nationals. According to historians: "Signed on May 6 1882, the Chinese Exclusion Act, which banned 'skilled and unskilled labourers and Chinese employed in mining' from entering the US for 10 years, was the first significant law restricting immigration to the country. It came at a time when the US was struggling with high unemployment and, although Chinese made up a very small segment of the country's workforce, they were nevertheless scape-goated for its social and economic woes. The law also placed restrictions on Chinese who were already in the US, forcing them to obtain certificates in order to re-enter if they left the country and banning them from securing citizenship. The act expired in 1892 but was extended for a further 10 years in the form of another the Geary Act. This placed additional restrictions on Chinese residents of the country, forcing them to register and to obtain a certificate of residence, without which they could be deported. This changed in 1943 with the Magnuson Act which allowed some Chinese immigration and for some Chinese already residing in the country to become naturalized citizens, but which maintained the ban on property and business ownership. This came at a time when China was a US ally during World War II. Second to this, was the **Jewish refugees ban during World War II by** *President Franklin D. Roosevelt.* As millions of people became refugees during World War II, US President Franklin D Roosevelt argued that refugees posed a serious threat to the country's national security. Drawing on fears that Nazi spies could be hiding among them, the country limited the number of German Jews who could be admitted to 26,000 annually. And it is estimated that for most of the Hitler era, less than 25 percent of that quota was actually filled. In one of the most notorious cases, the US turned away the St Louis ocean liner, which was carrying 937 passengers, almost all of whom are thought to have been Jewish, in June 1939. The ship was forced to return to Europe, where more than a quarter of its passengers are thought to have been killed in the Holocaust. Also in 1901, President William McKinley had been fatally shot by Leon Czolgosz, an American anarchist who was the son of Polish immigrants. The act which was also known as the Immigration Act of 1903 codified previous immigration law and, in addition to anarchists, added three other new classes of people who would be banned from entry: those with epilepsy, beggars and importers of prostitutes. The act marked the first time that individuals were banned for their political beliefs. The fourth on the list of such ban was the **Communists banned p**assed by *Congress on August 23, 1950, despite being vetoed by President Harry Truman.* The Internal Security Act of 1950 also known as the Subversive Activities Control Act of 1950 or the McCarran Act made it possible to deport any immigrants believed to be members of the Communist Party. Members of communist organisations, which were required to register, were also not allowed to become citizens. Although Truman opposed the law, stating that it "would make a mockery of our Bill of Rights". Sections of the act were ruled unconstitutional by the Supreme Court in 1993. But some parts of the act still stand. The fifth was the ban of the Iranians by *President Jimmy Carter, April 7, 1980. This happened following* the 1979 Iranian hostage crisis, during which the US embassy in Tehran was stormed and 52 Americans were held hostage for 444 days, American President Jimmy Carter cut diplomatic relations with and imposed sanctions on Iran. He also banned Iranians from entering the country. The sixth was the **Ban on HIV positive persons u**nder President Ronald Reagan, the US Public Health Service added Aids to its list of 'dangerous and contagious' diseases. Senator Jesse Helms' 'Helms Amendment' added HIV to the exclusion list. Specifically, in 1987, the US banned HIV positive persons from arriving in the US. The laws were influenced by homophobic and xenophobic sentiment towards Africans and minorities at the time, as well as a false belief that the HIV virus could be spread by physical or respiratory contact. Former US President Barack Obama lifted it in 2009, completing a process begun by President George W Bush" (Aljazeera, 2017).

The reaction in Trump's era however seems to be much more than the actual act of the immigration control policies declared. As tweeted by President Donald Trump (2017):

"When a country is no longer able to say who can, and who cannot, come in and out, especially for reasons of safety &.security. There is big trouble!" He furthered, "Interesting that certain Middle-Eastern countries agree with the ban. They know if certain people are allowed in, it's death and destruction!"

An overview of stated issues within Trump's executive order or visa ban, which is administratively referred to as: "Executive Order 13769, titled Protecting the Nation from Foreign Terrorist Entry into the United States, commonly known as the Muslim ban or the travel ban, was an executive order issued by United States President Donald Trump. Except for the extent to which it was blocked by various courts, it was in effect from 27 January 2017, until 16 March 2017, when it was superseded by Executive Order 13780. Executive Order 13769 lowered the number of refugees to be admitted into the United States in 2017 to 50,000, suspended the U.S. Refugee Admissions Program (USRAP) for 120 days, suspended the entry of Syrian refugees indefinitely, directed some cabinet secretaries to suspend entry of those whose countries do not meet adjudication standards under U.S. immigration law for 90 days, and included exceptions on a case-by-case basis. Homeland Security lists these countries as Iran, Iraq, Libya, Somalia, Sudan, Syria, and Yemen. More than 700 travelers were detained, and up to 60,000 visas were provisionally revoked. Immediately, there were numerous protests and legal challenges, with some calling it a 'Muslim ban' due to the fact that six of the affected countries had a Muslim majority. A nationwide temporary restraining order (TRO) was issued on 3 February 2017 in the case *Washington v. Trump*, which was upheld by the United States Court of Appeals for the Ninth Circuit on 9 February 2017. Consequently, the Department of Homeland Security (DHS) stopped enforcing portions of the order and the State Department re-validated visas that had been previously revoked. The order was criticized by members of Congress from both parties, universities, business leaders, Catholic bishops, top United Nations officials, a group of 40 Nobel laureates, Jewish organizations, 1,000 U.S. diplomats who signed a dissent cable, thousands of academics, and longstanding U.S. allies" *Bier (2017)*.

The constitutional ground upon which President Trump had relied before his Immigration ban policy declaration included some Acts of parliaments towards this achievement. In line with the Statutory authorization and related prohibitions: "Key provisions of executive orders 13769 and 13780 cite to paragraph (f) of Title 8 of the United States Code § 1182, which discusses inadmissible aliens. Paragraph (f) states thus: 'Whenever the President finds that the entry of any aliens or of any class of aliens into the United States would be detrimental to the interests of the United States, he may by proclamation, and for such period as he shall deem necessary, suspend the entry of all aliens or any class of aliens as immigrants or non-immigrants, or impose on the entry of aliens any restrictions he may deem to be appropriate.' The act that underlies this, known as the Immigration and Nationality Act of 1952 (a.k.a. the McCarran–Walter Act), was amended by the Immigration and Nationality Act of 1965 (a.k.a. the Hart–Celler Act), which included a provision stating: 'No person shall receive any preference or priority or be discriminated against in the issuance of an immigrant visa because of the person's race, sex, nationality, place of birth, or place of residence.' This language in the INA of 1965 is among the reasons District of Maryland Judge Chuang issued a temporary restraining order blocking Section 2(c) of Executive Order 13780" *(Diamond & Almasy (2017)*.

Further on this analysis, *Bier (2017)* argued through the Obama administrative restrictions and also referencing 1986 policy thus: "In 1986, the Visa Waiver Program was initiated by President

Ronald Reagan, allowing alien nationals of select countries to travel to the United States for up to 90 days without a visa, in return for reciprocal treatment of U.S. nationals. By 2016, the program had been extended to 38 countries. In 2015, Congress passed a Consolidated Appropriations Act to fund the government, and Obama signed the bill into law. The Visa Waiver Program Improvement and Terrorist Travel Prevention Act of 2015, which was previously passed by the House of Representatives as H.R. 158, was incorporated into the Consolidated Appropriations Act as Division O, Title II, Section 203. The Trump administration's executive order relied on H.R. 158, as enacted. The Visa Waiver Program Improvement and Terrorist Travel Prevention Act originally affected four countries: Iraq, Syria, and countries on the State Sponsors of Terrorism list (Iran and Sudan). Foreigners who were nationals of those countries, or who had visited those countries since 2011, were required to obtain a visa to enter the United States, even if they were nationals or dual nationals of the 38 countries participating in the Visa Waiver Program. Libya, Yemen, and Somalia were added later as 'countries of concern' by Secretary of Homeland Security Jeh Johnson during the Obama administration. The executive order refers to these countries as 'countries designated pursuant to Division O, Title II, Section 203 of the 2016 consolidated Appropriations Act.' Prior to this, in 2011, additional background checks were imposed on the nationals of Iraq. Trump's press secretary Sean Spicer however cited these existing restrictions as evidence that the executive order was based on outstanding policies saying that the seven targeted countries were 'put (...) first and foremost' by the Obama administration. Fact-checkers at PolitiFact.com, *The New York Times,* and *The Washington Post* said the Obama restrictions cannot be compared to this executive order because they were in response to a credible threat and were not a blanket ban on all individuals from those countries, and concluded that the Trump administration's statements about the Obama administration were misleading and false."

In the center of this debate about the United States' partial travel ban policy, Sean Keener, a profound traveler and tourist revealed the list of ten (10) toughest countries of the world to migrate to and ironically, there are predominantly same Muslim-nations who now struggle to get into America at all cost. In Sean (2017) analysis, "Most countries have a set of organized visa requirements to facilitate the entry of citizens of other countries for tourism, business, study, work, or retirement purposes. In countries where organized visa requirements are not the rule, getting a visa can confuse and frustrate even the well-seasoned traveler. Below is a list of the top 10 countries with the most difficult visa processes (in order of increasing difficulty)." In his explanation, he asserted as quoted: "I have included information on how to go about getting the visa and what people can expect after applying. It is most unreasonable to stay within these countries longer than the few days the short-term visa (or stamp) they issued to you lapses" he emphasized. These difficult countries however included:

10. Iran: "There are two main ways only you can get a visa to go to Iran as a tourist. The first route is travelling to Kish Island, Iran. Kish Island is a beautiful island located just off the coast of mainland Iran, surrounded by the crystal clear turquoise waters of the Persian Gulf. I went a couple of years ago, and it is definitely worth the trip. Passport holders of any country can travel to Kish Island without having to obtain a visa in advance. The easiest way to get there is to fly into Dubai International Airport and then transfer to the Kish Air flight to Kish Island. When you arrive in Kish Island, you will have to present your passport and take a series of fingerprints. The whole process takes about 30 minutes, and the immigration officials are friendly. 'Citizens of many countries can get a tourist visa on arrival at the airport in Tehran, valid for a stay of seven days. U.S. citizens; however, must arrange for a visa in advance.' The second way to get to Iran is to apply for a visa for mainland Iran, which will enable you to visit Tehran and other areas of mainland Iran. If you are planning to travel during the winter, Iran has some amazing ski resorts, no more than an hour's drive from Tehran. Citizens of many countries can get a tourist visa on arrival at the airport in Tehran, valid for a stay of seven days. U.S. citizens; however, must arrange for a visa in advance by applying through an accredited Iranian tour group."

9. Iraq: "For those wanting to travel to Iraq, the easiest and most viable option is to fly into Erbil, Iraq, an old town in the relatively stable Kurdistan Region of Iraq. Citizens of several countries, including the United States, European Union, Canada, Japan, or Australia, can obtain a free stamp upon arrival (good for a stay of 10 days)."

8. Somalia: "While independent travel to most of Somalia is dangerous and not advised, the autonomous northwestern part of Somalia, known as Somaliland, is open for the independent traveler. The easiest way to get to Somaliland is to fly into Addis Ababa, Ethiopia first and then head over to the Somaliland Liaison Office, located next to the Embassy of Mozambique."

7. North Korea: "The secret to getting into North Korea is that you will have to book a tour package through a travel agency accredited by the Government of North Korea. Although the process is difficult, it is not impossible. The steps required are as follows: (i) Book a tour package through a tour group accredited by the Government of North Korea. (ii) Fill out the online visa application. (Most tour groups will have an online application posted somewhere on their website). (iii) If you plan to enter North Korea via China, you will need to get a multiple entry visa for China first. Note that, in most instances, you will need to travel to Beijing and then go to Pyongyang from there. (iv) Once your visa has been processed, your tour group will usually provide you a location where you can go pick it up in Beijing. Sometimes, they may even pick up the visa for you on your behalf. If you are not entering North Korea via China, then you will not have to worry about picking up any documentation in Beijing."

6. Nauru: "Nauru is the world's smallest independent republic. It is a tiny country located in the South Pacific Ocean. You will find that the process of gathering the proper documentation to enter Nauru is quite bureaucratic and cumbersome. The process forgetting the visa to Nauru entails the following steps: (i) Book a flight to Nauru on Our Airline (formerly known as Air Nauru). (ii) Reserve a hotel room in Nauru (iii) E-mail the Nauru Consulate in Brisbane, Australia in order to obtain a visa form (iv) Fill out the visa form and return it to the Nauru Consulate so that they can send you your permission letter in order to enter Nauru (v) Carry this permission letter with you on your trip and present it upon landing in Nauru (vi) Hand over your passport to Immigration upon entry to Nauru. They will process your visa, which should be ready either same-day or next-day."

5. Sao Tome and Principe: "Sao Tome and Principe is a beautiful island country located off the west coast of Central Africa. Information on how to get a visa to go there is really tough to find if you do a search on the web, so I will spell out everything clearly for you below. There are two main ways to get a tourist visa for Sao Tome and Principe: Option 1: Contact a travel agent to do everything for you. Option 2: Apply through your local consulate/embassy. I advise you to select Option 1 and have a reputable Sao Tome and Principe travel agent process all the paperwork for you so that you don't have to go through the hassle of gathering a lot of documents to send off to the local embassy or consulate. The travel agent will likely request a copy of the first two pages of your passport and then e-mail or fax to you a formal permission form from the Ministry, authorizing you to enter Sao Tome and Principe without a visa. Be sure to bring this formal permission document with you, or you may not be allowed entry into the country."

4. Bhutan: "To get a tourist visa for Bhutan, you will need to go through a licensed tour operator, who will guide you through the process step-by-step. The process takes a great deal of time, but, once approved, you will have no trouble getting in."

3. Central African Republic: "The Central African Republic embassies and consulates have little to no presence on the web. In fact, the Embassy of the Central African Republic in Washington D.C. does not even have a website. The trick is to find the Embassy contact information (which you can find pretty easily doing a web search) and call them up to find out the latest paperwork and fees required."

2. Guinea-Bissau: "Guinea-Bissau does not have a consulate or embassy in either the United States or the United Kingdom. In 2007, in fact, the Embassy of Guinea-Bissau in Washington D.C. completely suspended operations. In order to get a visa to enter Guinea-Bissau, you will need to go to either Lisbon, Portugal and get it the same day (expensive option) or go to Ziguinchor, Senegal and get it at the Guinea Bissau Consulate (recommended option)."

1. Libya: "Libya is the toughest place to enter as a foreigner. Did you know that for several years prior to June 2010, Libya banned tourist visas for U.S. citizens? Libya had implemented similar bans in the past for citizens of various countries in Europe. (Note) 'Libya is the toughest place to enter as a foreigner.' The situation is volatile in this part of the world, but, if you are determined to add Libya to your bucket list, you need to know that, like North Korea, Libya requires tourists to apply for a visa through a licensed tour operator. If you do a search online, you will find several reputable Libya tour agencies. After booking a tour, you will be asked to send a scanned copy of your passport, your dates of travel, return ticket, personal contact information, and other information that is typical for getting visas for other countries. The tour agency in Libya has the responsibility for filing all of your paperwork with the Libya Immigration Department, who will issue a letter (in Arabic) that you will need to bring with you on your trip. This letter is your official authorization for a visa upon entry into Libya."

Other countries with hard-to-get visas, according to him included: **"Turkmenistan, Equatorial Guinea and Cuba (SPECIFICALLY, CUBA'S VISA IS VERY HARD TO GET FOR U.S. CITIZENS)"**

(Source: Addison Sears-Collins, 2015; represented by Sean Keener, 2017. Retrieved from: http://www.bootsnall.com/articles/12-10/top-10-toughest-countries-to-get-into.html).

Ironically, the faces behind most of the popular mass rallies that have been acclaimed to be the people's voices against Visa-Ban-Policies can be found through the list below. The list of such organizations included:

(i)   The Muslim Association of Britain,

(ii)   The Muslim Engagement and Development,

(iii)   The Muslim Council of Britain,

(iv)   The CND,

(v)   The Friends of Al-Aqsa, and

(vi)   The People's Assembly Against Austerity and Help Refugees Worldwide.

5.2   DACA and Donald Trump's Position on the Dreamers

The premise upon which Trump's declaration of DACA cancellation is based stems from this fact stated below:

"After becoming president, Trump said he wanted to 'work something out' for the Dreamers. 'We don't want to hurt those kids,' he said. 'We love the Dreamers.' On the day the end of DACA was announced, he said: 'I have advised the department of homeland security that DACA recipients are not enforcement priorities unless they are criminals, are involved in criminal activity, or are members of a gang" *(Kopan, 2017)*.

Going by this intention, it should be understood that President Donald Trump's cancellation declaration of DACA program with the instructions issued out to the law makers to constitutionalize the legal stay of DACA beneficiaries is clearly to help these 'Dreamers' as they are fondly called and not to harm them. The key reason for this assertion is because the so called DACA program in itself has never been helpful to the beneficiary. It has no future for them. DACA policy can only afford the beneficiary the privilege to live, school, work and earn income legally within the United States through the Homeland security's issuance of Employment Authorization Documents to the beneficiaries. But for those who have lived long enough within the United States, they know better that anyone who is a mere holder of Employment Authorization Document (EAD) within the United States faces numerous limitations relating to career development and professional-job opportunities. To start with, such status has no definite classification under the United States' categories of ranking toward accessing opportunities that are available within the country. The order of recognition has remained:

1. The citizens (Born or Naturalized). Where the citizens by birth has limitless opportunities including the potency to becoming the President of the United States. A naturalized citizen can never.

2. The United States' Nationals are ranked second.

3. The Green Card holders

4. Other forms of status that are: refugees or Asylum related and

5. The holder of mere Employment Authorization Documents called EAD which is the category these 'Dreamers" currently belong.

The truth those who are agitating for non-cancellation of this policy wouldn't tell the world is that these "Dreamers" currently lack so many opportunities ranging from career and developmental opportunities under the EAD category they belong. Many meaningful career related jobs and positions are only for citizens and green card holders. EAD carriers are clearly restricted. A survey of the kind of jobs prevalent among the so called "Dreamers" under this DACA status are casual jobs such as cleaners, janitors, group home opportunities as Direct Support staff, laborers and a host of other casual jobs regardless of their educational status. This is because many employers with established and career driven positions only give such positions to Citizens and Green card holders whom they know will not have issues with renewal of legal stay which these DACA "dreamers" struggle with from time to time and, when their work authorization expires. More so, in the United States of today as it stands, you can never be able to work in certain government agencies such as CIA, FBI, the Police or in other law enforcement positions except you are citizens. Some other government agencies in some states may consider Green card holders for correction services but the holders of these other form of legal stay within which the DACA's Dreamers belong are currently differentiated against, despite their long years of legal residency within the United States. The worse situation for DACA beneficiaries is due to the reality in the fact that there is no hope of building through this status to acquire green card or become citizens. In fact, holders of asylum status and holders of refugee status have better hope than DACA dreamers. Both refugees and asylees can follow through those statuses to acquire green card and become citizens but such provisions are not contained in DACA policy or executive program. Needless to reiterate that in DACA situation, there is no future of graduation from the EAD status or category.

This is considered as the evil in the DACA policy which this cancellation policy will correct if given due attention and, if the issues at stake are well understood. Reliably, President Trump has repeated emphasized that he is open to accord these "Dreamers" the citizenship status which they can never be able to dream of, as dreamers under DACA. There is nothing dreaming about the dreamers therefore as long as they remain under DACA program. The holders of DACA should therefore be well informed that Trump is not their problem, the law makers are.

According to *Duke (2017)*, "the Deferred Action for Childhood Arrivals (DACA) was an American immigration policy that allowed some individuals who entered the country as minors, and had either entered or remained in the country illegally, to receive a renewable two-year period of deferred action from deportation and to be eligible for a work permit. As of 2017, approximately 800,000 individuals were enrolled in the program created by DACA." In Kapan (2017)'s elaborate report on DACA he explained as follow:

"DACA is a federal government program created in 2012 under Barack Obama to allow people brought to the US as children, and who have been living illegally, the temporary right to live, study and work in America. Those applying are vetted for any criminal history or threat to national security and must be students or have completed school or military service. If they pass vetting, action to deport them is deferred for two years, with a chance to renew, and they become eligible for basics like a driving license, college enrollment or a work permit. Those protected under DACA are known as 'Dreamers' and as at the time Trump announced his decision to rescind the program, about 787,580 had been granted approval. To apply, they must have been younger than 31 on 15 June 2012, when the program began, and 'undocumented,' lacking legal immigration status. They must have arrived in the US before turning 16 and lived there continuously since June 2007. Most Dreamers are from Mexico, El Salvador, Guatemala and Honduras and the largest numbers live in California, Texas, Florida and New York. They range in age from 15 to 36, according to the White House sources."

He further that:

"The DACA program was a compromise devised by the Obama administration after Congress failed to pass the so called Development, Relief and Education for Alien Minors (Dream) Act, which would have offered those who had arrived illegally as children the chance of permanent legal residency. The bipartisan act was introduced in 2001 and has repeatedly failed to pass" Kapan (2017).

From the forgoing, it appears President Donald Trump's interest; which should interest the concerned beneficiaries; is the President's push to force the law makers to do their job and pass the law that can legalize the status of DACA beneficiaries. The job of the executive is to sign whatever the law makers pass into law so that there can be true dreams for these dreamers to smile home about. This was the exact marching order the president issued out to the law makers as at September, 2017 while declaring the suspension of the program.

5.3 Issues In Illegal Migration, Refugees And The Wall At Mexican Border

Picture 5.3.1: Prototype for US-Mexico Border Wall
(Source: https://www.cnbc.com/2017/10/24/prototypes-for-us-mexico-border

wall-unveiled.html)

Wall-building has been one of the traditional ways of imposing physical restriction and security along the border line over the years. Ancient cities and communities have used this security feature tremendously to prevent undue invasions and infiltration into their society. They equally used this pattern of restriction to make border-line policing easier.

The border of Mexico has been largely pin pointed as the sure route into the United States for most refugees or migrants who cannot attain American visa legally. However, the major problem associated with this has been that the larger percentage of migrants who strive to come into the United States through this route are largely from African countries next to Mexican population. Saeed (2017) captured the danger such migrants from Africa have constantly been exposed to, thus: "More than 22,500 migrants have reportedly died or disappeared globally since 2014 – more than half of them perishing while attempting to cross the Mediterranean, according to a study by the International Organization for Migration (IOM). A clampdown on Europe's eastern borders has forced migrants to choose more dangerous routes as the death toll in the Mediterranean continues to rise despite a drop in the overall number of arrivals, data compiled by the UN's migration agency shows. 'While overall numbers of migrants attempting to cross the Mediterranean by the eastern route were reduced significantly in 2016 by the EU-Turkey deal, death rates have increased to 2.1 per 100 in 2017, relative to

1.2 in 2016,' reads the IOM report. Part of this rise is due to the greater proportion of migrants now taking the most dangerous route – that across the central Mediterranean – such that 1 in 49 migrants now died on this route in 2016." Since 2014, more deaths have been documented on this route than any other migration route in the world. In the first half of this year, the IOM said at least 3,110 migrants have died or disappeared globally, which is lower than the figure in 2016 (4,348), but the risk of dying has increased in the Mediterranean even though fewer migrants crossed into Europe. More than 1,300 migrants rescued from Mediterranean in single day. The central Mediterranean route, ending at Lampedusa or the main island of Sicily, accounts only for about a quarter of almost 1.5 million people who have arrived since 2014 on all routes, but for 88% of all migrant deaths in the Mediterranean," it said.

Recently, Amnesty International criticized Italy for taking measures to keep migrants away from its shores, which it said leads "in their arbitrary detention in centres where they are at almost certain risk of torture, rape and even of being killed". "The IOM's report also complained about smugglers in Libya and Italy increasingly using less seaworthy vessels. Jean-Guy Vataux, head of mission in Libya for Médecins Sans Frontières, told the Guardian nearly all the people rescued from drowning in the Mediterranean have been 'exposed to an alarming level of violence and exploitation: kidnap for ransom, forced labour, sexual violence and enforced prostitution, being kept in captivity or detained arbitrarily.' According to Vataux, the majority of migrants in

Libya live clandestinely 'under the yoke of smugglers or – for the most unlucky – kidnapping organisations."

He added: "Migrants going through Libya to reach Europe are facing impossible choices: getting on a boat is very risky, many die before they reach the European coast or a rescue ship. Remaining in Libya, whether in detention centres run by the administration or a criminal organisation, exposes them to unbelievable levels of violence and exploitation.

There are more challenges to their options aside attempting to follow through or safe passage to other Mediterranean countries. Restrictions on the eastern route meant the number of arrivals in countries such as Croatia, Serbia and Macedonia had dramatically dropped. The three countries, which are not a part of the EU border-free Schengen zone, restricted migrants' access in late 2015. In the first half of this year, at least seven migrants have died of hypothermia during the winter months in the western Balkans. The International Committee of the Red Cross (ICRC) has recently published a report warning of the dangers in the route. A mother and son who successfully crossed the Evros river – along the border between Turkey and Greece – both later died of hypothermia. More than 120,000 people have arrived in Europe by sea in 2016 – most departed from Libya bound for Italy, from Turkey bound for Greece or, more recently, from Morocco bound for Spain. About 82% of all migrants were travelling to Italy from Libya. In June, the Italian coastguard rescued about 5,000 people in one day in the Mediterranean. The IOM report covers the period from January 2014 to the end of June and thus does not reflect the recent developments in Myanmar, where atrocities against the country's Rohingya Muslim minority has led to an exodus of thousands to neighbouring Bangladesh. The IOM report, titled Fatal Journeys, has been compiled by the Berlin-based Global Migration Data Analysis Centre (GMDAC). It is the only existing database on migrant deaths at the global level, collected through various means including official records, medical examiners and media reports. Ann Singleton, senior research fellow at the University of Bristol's school for policy studies, said: 'For the families left behind it could make a real difference if they are able to find more information on their missing relatives. Better data on migrant fatalities can also help inform policies aimed at reducing migrant deaths.' Global figures for the first half of 2017 show that northern Africa also had high fatalities and disappearances, with at least 225 recorded deaths. The majority of incidents occurred along routes from western Africa and the Horn of Africa towards Libya and Egypt. Sickness and violence are the main cause of death in those cases."

It was further narrated through the report that: "At least 150 deaths were also recorded in the US-Mexico border crossings since January. 'Along the border, irregular migrants avoid coming into contact with authorities in well-patrolled areas and are often forced to cross natural hazards such as the desert of Arizona or the fast-running Rio Grande river,' IOM said. More people have died attempting to cross the border compared with last year despite an ease in border apprehensions of migrants. Recent clampdowns on the Libya-Italy route have also led to the increase in attempts to reach the continent via Morocco. The IOM has said the number of people arriving in Spain by sea this year is likely to outnumber the number arriving in Greece. Francesca Friz Prguda, UNHCR representative in Spain, who recently visited the port cities of Tarifa and Algeciras, where refugees are arriving almost daily after crossing the strait of Gibraltar from Morocco, said Spain was underprepared and lacked an integrated national strategy. More than 14,000 migrants have arrived by sea – a 90% increase compared with last year. Arrivals in Andalusian ports have tripled. 'While this is really not an emergency situation if you compare it to Italy, there are no adequate structures and procedures in place to deal even with the current level, let alone with more arrivals,' she said. 'It's a myth to assume that people arriving here are all economic migrants, sub-Saharan Africa is one of the most refugee-producing regions in the world, so even statistically there's a likelihood that these mixed flows are refugees travelling,' she said. 'A lot of media have not dealt with the issue in a very responsible way, talking about avalanches and storms, flood, and God knows what – there's a clearly a perception which doesn't seem to sufficiently understand that first there are many refugee-producing countries in sub-Saharan Africa" she added.

Picture 5.3.2: **Pictorial sample of migrants in Mediterranean Sea I**

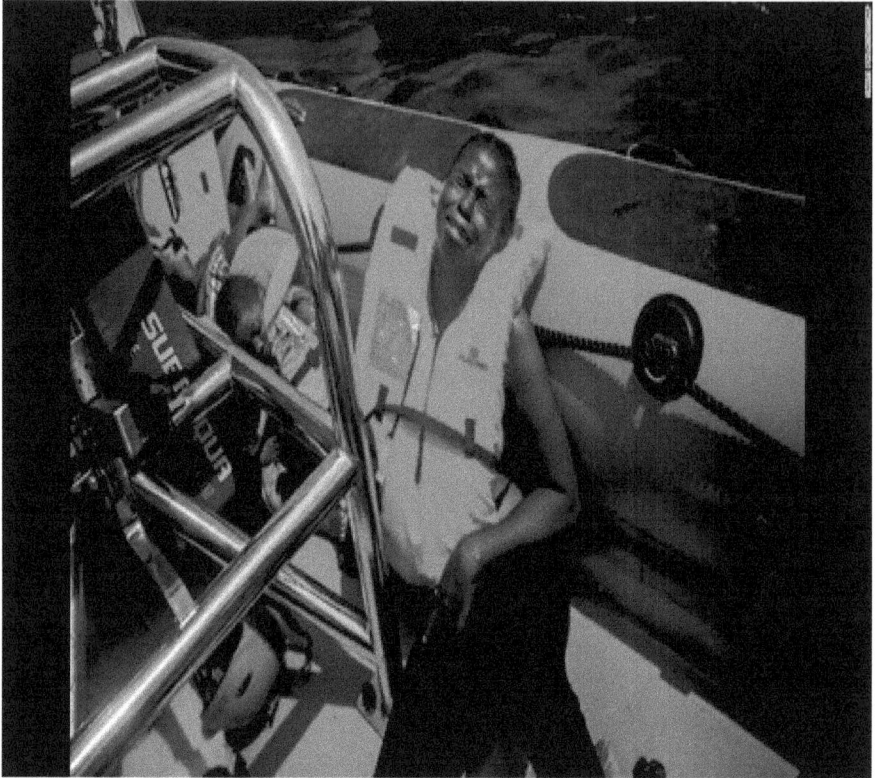

(Source: https://www.cnn.com/2015/09/03/world/gallery/europes-refugee-crisis/index.html)

Picture 5.3.3: **Pictorial sample of migrants in Mediterranean Sea II**

(Source: https://www.cnn.com/2015/09/03/world/gallery/europes-refugee-crisis/index.html)

Picture 5.3.4:   **Pictorial sample of migrants in Mediterranean Sea III**

(Source: https://www.cnn.com/2015/09/03/world/gallery/europes-refugee-crisis/index.html)

Picture 5.3.5: **Pictorial sample of migrants in Mediterranean Sea IV**

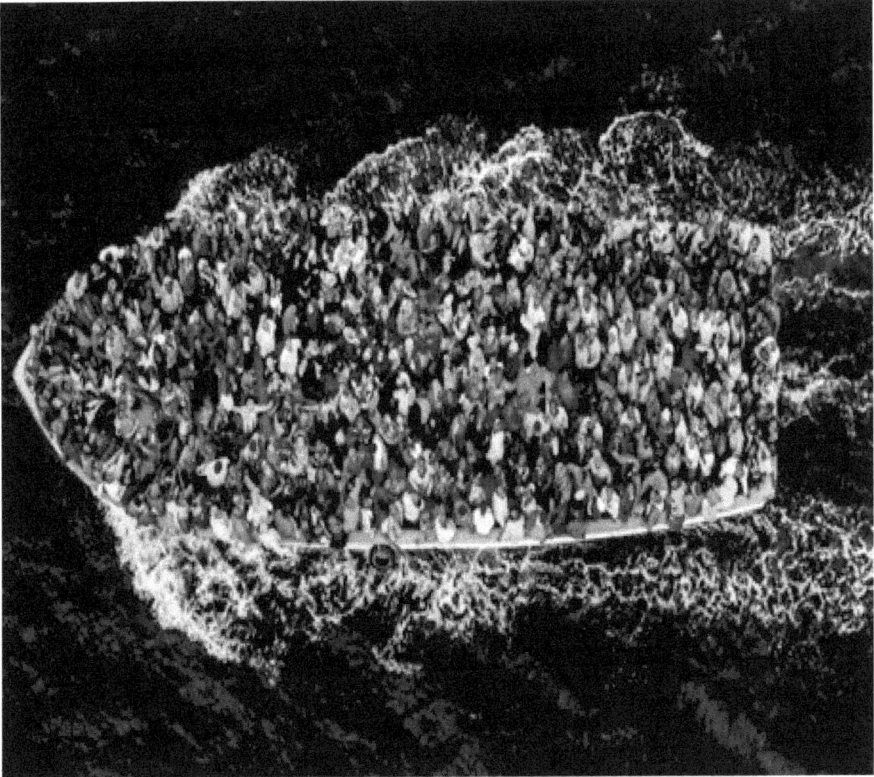

Picture 5.3.6: **Pictorial sample of migrants through Mexico-border Desert to United States I**

(Source: https://sputniknews.com/latam/201703171051669949-mexico-immigrants-tranfer-funds-bank-accounts/)

Picture 5.3.7:   **Picto Mexico-border Desert to United Mexico-border Desert to United States II'**

(Source:

https://www.google.com/
search?q=pictures+of+migrants+through+mexico+deserts&
tbm=isch&source=iu&ictx=1&fir=XhZJxMo37k4yqM%
253A%252CRrB9GKtc6b54SM%252C_&
usg= 9mx-zk_hRF_KqA881cUcz-
Cf1fc%3D&sa=X&ved=0ahUKEwipsoqw3_jYAhWD6IMKHRooCP
4Q9QEILTAC#imgrc=8ZPUWkz5tmLeUM:&spf=1517076595119)

On arrival in Europe, these migrants followed through the journey to Mexico usually so as to be able to gain entrance into the United States through Mexican border since they believe most European territories have stringent immigration laws and lesser humanitarian policies than USA.

Year in, year out, America has religiously passed into its own system, people who shared nothing in common with the principles that established its foundation in the name of refugee program. According to statistics:

"The United States runs the world's largest refugee resettlement program. Not only this, European countries who are already wary of welcoming more Syrian refugees, asylum seekers and migrants from Iraq, Eritrea, and elsewhere beckoned the USA to absorb them. (**The United States had resettled hundreds of thousand refugees from around the world).** And approximately 2,000 Syrian refugees were specifically settled in as of October, 2015 since the start of civil war in Syria in 2011. From that point forward, the annual ceiling on U.S. refugee admissions has ranged from 85,000 for the fiscal year that began October 1, 2015 and to 100,000 the following year, up from 70,000 for the fiscal year that ended September 30, 2015" (Migration Policy Institute, 2015).

Above clearly demonstrated the magnanimity and humanitarian disposition of the United States and this has been its character from ages. However, when the founding fathers of America were promulgating their immigration laws in centuries past; they never envisaged today's chaotic world. They had only opined that America could be religiously passive for purposes of peaceful co-existence. But in today's 21st century world, the story has changed. People who were attacked by September 11 terrorist incident didn't have to do anything wrong to Osama Bin Ladden before he attacked and killed them. People who have been bombed at train stations, at airports and major other strategic locations within and around the United States didn't have to do anything personal to offend their bombers before they were bombed. The world indeed has changed. So also must the instruments of co-existence within it be reviewed. Laws and policies must be reviewed not because the country does not want to be nice to others, but because the country cares enough for the safety, security and considerable peace of mind of its own citizens within its territory.

Issues in immigration and migration are so numerous and complex such that the writer of this book deems it important to issue passionate advice to students of wisdom to understand with the stance of the current government on immigration and migration, rather than being parochial about such. Since this whole battle relates more with the future of America and the kind of society the current generation cares to leave behind for their unborn children to inherit. For instance, Americans who are Christians today can go to their churches and worship centers peacefully without threats of bombing because the internal fanatics within it are yet to grow and accumulate to the break-loose point. Countries that have accumulated fanatics long enough through careless policies of the years past are in better position to explain what it feels like to go to places of worship with security guards and police, just to be sure they can be protected in the course of service. The only way to curb more violence-belief-culture coming into America therefore is to look critically into its immigration policies and enable it to suit the tempo of time. By this, such policies can be able to define the kind of people America's city-gate can be opened to periodically.

It is public knowledge however that the past internal terrorists activities recorded in America were mostly carried out by the children of those whom America as a nation harbors through humanitarian sympathy. Though the same Americans; whose income taxes are being used to harbor them; cannot be allowed to live in safety in some of the countries where those fanatics came from. For students of wisdom once more, it has been said, if you cannot save others, at least, please, save yourself.

Let this wisdom sinks furthermore, that it is easier to fight the enemies without but as for the enemies within, such enemies have higher capacity to destabilize the host, no matter the level of security network. Incidents of the past have proven this. It is therefore sufficient to assert that Donald Trump is preserving the future of the great America. **The best its citizens can do is to let him, if they can't help him.**

CHAPTER SIX

6.0 ILLEGAL IMMIGRANTS AND THE CAPITALIST-COMPANIES' REAP-OFF IN U.S.

An Illegal immigrant or undocumented immigrant as popularly referred is a foreign national who is living without authorization in a country where he/se is not a citizen. Lots of debates have come up on issues of undocumented immigrants both politically and in the academic. These debates have always been back and forth. They have always been pros and cons with some groups decrying the situation and rejecting the development with stern position while others have been more lenient and considerate with the situation. Whatever the positions of the debaters have been however, the reality of time indicates that the issue of undocumented immigrant is a real one. In fact the statistics of such nationals streams in thousands from communities to communities and from one state to another within the United States.

One of the main issues derived in the course of argument and counter argument on undocumented immigrants, nevertheless, is the reap-off that goes with it. The presence of undocumented or illegal immigrants has contributed immensely to the increasing reap-off of the many business owners capitalists. The availability of undocumented immigrants is to the advantage of that group of people. It has helped in the continuing human/labor exploitation which many human right activists fought against over decades at the risk of imprisonment. Not only this, availability of undocumented immigrants has continued to extend the continuity of certain modern day en-slavery characteristics. An average undocumented person has limited choices to what he or she can say 'No' to. The availability has strengthened prostitutions for survival in situation where personalities involved are women. It has encouraged dehumanization practices since many of the undocumented persons are usually subject to whatever offers anyone who tries to assist them offers. It has lead to the continued imprisonment of ordinary innocent souls who naturally may not have tendencies to committing crimes but who may have run into criminal syndicates for assistance in the course of seeking help to live in a foreign land.

The risk-list is long but of peculiar interest on such list, is the reap-offer syndrome which has been one of the reasons many business-owners and capitalists who benefit largely from this situation fight the government any time immigration policies get tougher. In fact, many scholars have argued that neither the government nor the undocumented immigrants themselves are benefitting from this cheap labor reap-off. The only beneficiaries have been the capitalist business owners who try to maximize profit through cheap labors. Although, many social activists who are aware of this reap-off/loophole have term it to be the modern day approach to re-enslaving the African migrants within the European territories and indeed the United States once more, but unfortunately, they have not been able to do much about it. Neither do they have a straight answer to addressing such issue since the 'subjects' of the reap-off (the illegal immigrants) have continued to troop in from their various third world economies into the European territories on their own.

Additionally, the more reason many opinionists believe it will be very difficult to end illegal immigrants or undocumented immigrants activities is because those who are benefiting from the reap-off will always be at the fore-front of maintaining the system. They will always sponsor opinions against any government's move to hamper it. They will always lure other innocent citizens who benefit nothing from such activities to join forces against the stoppage of the activities. Since, this is a business-line, such capitalists do not only kick against the anti-illegal immigrant policies but they romance with the law-makers to move against it too. Since there will always be a synergy among the various societal elites, be it political or economic, to improve their areas of advantages over the ordinary citizens.

Robert Shiller attempted to summarize the reap-off debates on undocumented immigrants when he wrote: "In summary, the immigration surplus stems from the increase in the return to capital that result from the increased supply of labor and the subsequent fall in wages.

Natives who own more capital will receive more income from the immigration surplus than natives who own less capital, who can consequently be adversely affected. The economic winners from rising illegal immigrants' levels are closely associated with the establishment wing: 'businesses and landowners and investors,' as Robert noted. It is just this wing that Trump ran against during the primaries. The engagement of illegal immigrants raises the overall income of the capitalist companies that absorbs them: the immigration surplus through the engagement of undocumented immigrants. This surplus is directly related to the degree to which immigration changes wages and returns to capital. In the simplest models, the more wages decline, the larger the surplus" (Robert, 2016).

Below reveals the position of Donald Trump and Hillary Clinton on undocumented immigrants in the course of their presidential debates in 2016.

According to Donald Trump on: 'How to Make America Great Again' slogan:

"I want good people to come here from all over the world, but I want them to do so legally. We can expedite the process, we can reward achievement and excellence, but we have to respect the legal process. And those people who take advantage of the system and come here illegally should never enjoy the benefits of being a resident — or citizen — of this nation. So I am against any path to citizenship for undocumented workers or anyone else who is in this country illegally. They should — and need to — go home and get in line."

Clinton was more succinct:

"If you work hard, if you love this country, if you contribute to it, and want nothing more than to build a good future for yourselves and your children, we should give you a way to come forward and become a citizen. And you know what? The majority of Americans agree. They know it's the right thing to do."

(Source: Keith (2016) Capitalist reap-off. Retrieved from: https://www.nytimes.com/2016/09/29/

opinion/campaign-stops/what-does-immigration-actually-cost-us.html)

CHAPTER SEVEN

7.0 AMERICA AND THE WORLD POLITICS IN DONALD TRUMP ERA

Under Donald Trump's America, many world leaders have learnt to absorb shocks. These shocks have translated to their less-public reactions on international matters concerning America and her new Presidency. These shocks have reflected in practical controls of their internal behaviors that could have influence on some international factors. These shocks have reflected in their awareness of the reality of new position of American leadership on zero tolerance for mediocrity. Since America's new position now frown at the possibility of some countries causing internal troubles (such as: over-population through unguided reproduction; aiding and abetting terrorism; as well as the problem of self-destruction through religious overzealousness and violent preaching) within itself while hoping to offload their internal mess into the United States as soon as it becomes a real mess. No doubt, there is a total change of direction to the usual approach to world politics under Donald Trump's America. This direction, in accordance to Trump campaign's slogan of "America-First" has ranked the priority of the United States in the order of:

(i) First to be protected against external attacks, which she is demonstrating through the reviews of its laws on security and influx.

(ii) First to be considered through her processes of bilateral and multi-lateral relations.

(iii) First to be considered through its positions on international issues in such a way that the country does not, any longer, burn its own arms while trying to warm the fingers of others.

(iv) First to be considered by not over-taxing its own working class in order to be able to import the terrorism that may destroy its own internal safety later

(v) First to be considered by realizing the need to take care of the future by checking the unguided activities of today among others.

It is so saddened that America as a nation is heavily indebted. This is not all; the system is also getting the younger generation robe in through what is referred as student loans, which is summarily, students' indebtedness. An average American child who went through educational institution is heavily indebted before he/she even thinks of gaining employment. Meanwhile, the same country kept borrowing more money in the past to sink such fund into other nations who hardly care about its existence or survival. In the words of Make Lemonade, "there are over 44 million borrowers with over $1.3 trillion in student loan debt, and the average student in the Class of 2016, for instance, has $37,172 in student loan debt" (Zack, 2017). Even in relation to social security, United States was already running red to take care of its own citizen. James (2017) reflected on this development thus: "Social Security paid out $905 billion last year (2016), almost one quarter of the U.S. government's expenditures, according to the Social Security Trustees report. Since 2010, America's largest government program has been cash flow negative, meaning that taxes and contributions no longer cover benefits. Last year the deficit covered by interest on the Trust Fund was almost $75 billion, and by 2020 the Trust Fund itself will start to be drawn down....President George W. Bush was the last to make a serious attempt to fix Social Security 12 years ago." Going by this re-prioritization policy of President Donald Trump however, the nation look good to save so much financially following the policy measures within the little time the current government came into office. According to New York Times (2017) **"Savings from reductions in war funding (only) is estimated to $593 billion. (This will be done by) p**hasing down the Defense Department's Overseas Contingency Operations fund, an off-budget spending account that is used to fund wars, saves some more money." In fact, limiting Trump's income saving to tax reform alone, it has been speculated according to: Andrew (2017), "'Typical' Household will save $4,000 with Tax Reform." This is equally important to the revitalization of US economy. In the past decades, America US economy was the leading economy in the world but not any more in recent years, the nation has been so distracted through accumulation of external exigencies and financial burdens upon itself while its own domestic economy degenerated; while its own internal infrastructures decayed and deepened in dilapidation, aside its growing financial indebtedness. Little wonder why the system continued to over-tax its working class.

Eliot (2017) captured some other messy situations inherited by Donald Trump's Presidency due to faulty foreign policies of the past, more accurately, when he wrote, "Donald Trump was right. He inherited a mess. In January 2017, American foreign policy was, if not in crisis, in big trouble. Strong forces were putting stress on the old global political order: the rise of China to a power with more than half the productive capacity of the United States (and defense spending to match); the partial recovery of a resentful Russia under a skilled autocrat; the discrediting of Western elites by the financial crash of 2008, followed by roiling populist waves; a turbulent Middle East and economic dislocations worldwide. An American leadership that had partly discredited itself over the past generation compounded these problems. The Bush administration's war against jihadist Islam had been undermined by reports of mistreatment and torture; its Afghan campaign had been inconclusive; its invasion of Iraq had been deeply compromised by what turned out to be a false premise and three years of initial mismanagement. The Obama administration's policy of retrenchment (described by a White House official as 'leading from behind') made matters worse. The United States was generally passive as a war that caused some half a million deaths raged in Syria. The ripples of the conflict reached far into Europe, as some 5 million Syrians fled the country. A red line about the use of chemical weapons turned pale pink and vanished, as Iran and Russia expanded their presence and influence in Syria ever more brazenly. A debilitating freeze in defense spending, meanwhile, left two-thirds of U.S. Army maneuver brigades unready to fight and Air Force pilots unready to fly in combat. These circumstances would have caused severe headaches for (any) competent and sophisticated successor."

CHAPTER EIGHT

8.0 ANALYSIS OF SOME FOREIGN POLICIES UNDER DONALD TRUMP'S PRESIDENCY

A country's foreign policy, in Christopher's (2003) word "is also called **foreign relations or foreign affairs policy**, consists of self-interest strategies chosen by the state to safeguard its national interests and to achieve goals within its international relations milieu." Simply put, it is a policy pursued by a nation in its dealings with other nations and, such policies are designed to achieve a particular country's national objectives. This means all countries around the world design their individual policies in line with their own individual targeted objectives. Self-analytically to imply that such individual country puts the interest of their nation first while formulating policy-directions towards their own socio-political and economic development.

America's foreign policy has been well defined however and, according to Norton & Company (2018): "American foreign policy has been and will continue to be about the *dynamics of choice*. One set of these choices is about foreign policy strategy – of what the national interest is and how best to achieve it. The other set of these choices is about *foreign policy politics* – of which institutions and actors within the American political system play what roles and have how much influence. Setting *process of choice* while foreign policy politics is the *process of choice*. Foreign policy strategy choices are made within the context of the international system. The international system, according to international relations theory, is characterized by three guiding principles: (i) Anarchy (ii) System structure based on the distribution of power and (iii) The structural position of states within the international system. Following the national interest is the essence of the choices to be made in a nation's foreign policy. The US national interest can be defined by four core goals: (i) Power (ii) Peace (iii) Prosperity and (iv) Principles. Power is the key requirement for the most basic goal of foreign policy – self defense and the preservation of national independence and territory. The *realist* school of international relations most emphasizes the objective of power. Power is key to maintain a strong defense and credible deterrence. The principle foreign policy strategies that follow from the realist line of reasoning are largely coercive ones. In a certain sense, all four of the national interest objectives ultimately are about achieving Peace. *International Institutionalism* stresses the importance of peace and promotes two types of foreign policy strategies. International Institutionalists see cooperation as viable between states and stress the importance of international institutions as the basis for 'sustained cooperation.' Foreign policies motivated by the goal of *Prosperity* give high priority to the economic national interest. One school of thought regarding American economic interests emphasizes, through foreign policy, the potential general economic benefit to the nation. The second school of thought sees American foreign policy as dominated by and serving the interests of capitalism, such as multinational corporations. This school of thought often results in imperialist or neocolonialist policies. The fourth core goal, *Principles*, involves the values, ideas, and beliefs that the US has claimed to stand for in the world. Democratic Idealism emphasizes the principles rooted in American history and holds two central tenets about American foreign policy: 'right' is to be chosen over 'might' and in the long run, 'right' makes for 'might.' At times, the 4P's are complementary."

The company further stated that, "During the Persian Gulf War all of the 4P's were served in some way. Likewise, the Marshall Plan was able to achieve the goals of peace, power, and prosperity. In other instances, however, trade-offs must be made between the 4P's. Finally, in some cases, the foreign policy debate is less about which P should take priority and more about a deep dissensus over the basic nature of the national interest. This is evidenced by the debate surrounding the 2003 Iraq War" (Norton & Company, 2018).

In the pursuit of the above, Donald Trump has rolled out a number of foreign policies within the short period he has been in office. Majority of these policies have attracted serious and massive reactions, both within and outside the shores of the United States. Prominent among these policies are: reviews of bilateral relations and war against terrorism or terrorist groups etc.

8.1 Jerusalem: Trump's Declaration and the Battle of Religions

According to Harvey (2000), "religion is a collection of cultural systems, beliefs and world views that establishes symbols that relate humanity to spirituality and, sometimes to moral values. While religion is hard to define, one standard model of religion, used in religious studies courses, was proposed by Clifford Geertz, who simply called it a 'cultural system.' A critique of Geertz's model by Talal Asad categorized religion as 'an anthropological category.' Many religions have narratives, symbols, traditions and sacred histories that are intended to give meaning to life or to explain the origin of life or the universe. They tend to derive morality, ethics, religious laws, or a preferred lifestyle from their ideas about the cosmos and human nature. According to some estimates, there are roughly 4,200 religions in the world. The word religion is sometimes used interchangeably with 'faith' or 'belief system,' but religion differs from private belief in that it has a public aspect. Most religions have organized behaviours, including clerical hierarchies, a definition of what constitutes adherence or membership, congregations of laity, regular meetings or services for the purposes of veneration of a deity or for prayer, holy places (either natural or architectural) or religious texts. Certain religions also have a sacred language often used in liturgical services. The practice of a religion may also include sermons, commemoration of the activities of a god or gods, sacrifices, festivals, feasts, trance, initiations, funerals, marriages, meditation, music, art, dance, public service or other aspects of human culture. He furthered that "Religious beliefs have also been used to explain parapsychological phenomena such as out-of-body experiences, near-death experiences and reincarnation, along with many other paranormal experiences."

He further that: "Some academics studying the subject have divided religions into three broad categories: world religions, a term which refers to trans-cultural, international faiths; indigenous religions, which refers to smaller, culture-specific or nation-specific religious groups; and new religious movements, which refers to recently developed faiths. One modern academic theory of religion, social constructionism, says that religion is a modern concept that suggests all spiritual practice and worship follows a model similar to the Abrahamic religions as an orientation system that helps to interpret reality and define human beings. Thus, religion, as a concept, has been applied inappropriately to non-Western cultures that are not based upon such systems, or in which these systems are a substantially simpler construct" (Harvey, 2000).

Whether frantically or silently, **the battle over Jerusalem is a religion one.** "Many centuries ago,' the Jews claimed that 'the God of the Christian had already claimed Jerusalem as His as it is written in the Holy Bible:"

"But I HAVE CHOSEN JERUSALEM, that My Name might be there; and have chosen David to be over my people Israel." (2 Chronicles 6:6)

This battle over Jerusalem has proven a point and the point remains that; those who wait for problems and wars to occur before learning proactive lessons always have their wounds to lick. This must have been the case with the people of Jerusalem before they actually lost their territory to strangers who now lay claims to it. *Historians, analysts and other religious writers have written and decried the fear about Islamists ploy to take over the world but only few persons have paid attention to this. According to a religious writer, Modupe Olojo, who wrote:*

"when will the world WAKE UP TO HOW ISLAMISTS PLAN TO ISLAMIZE THE WORLD IN CENTURIES AFTER US? When will

the intellectuals read the lines of the rhythms before it becomes a song? Everywhere that there has been religious and socio-humanitarian chaos in the world, it is worth to check the patterns. First, a reasonable percentage of the nationals of those nations are Islamists and I say this without prejudice or bias to the religion. Rather, I attempt to communicate with the objectivity of reality. It is definitely important to note there are hundreds of religions and varying belief systems in many countries of the world today aside the dominant Christianity and Islam. But only Islam will keep us all on red alert, why? Of course, over decades, the world has known no rest because of what some section of human beings believed in, which they considered superior to whatever the rest of the world believes. Second, the principle of Islamization teaches polygamy and unguided reproduction or mass-production of children. Simply, the followers of this religion are encouraged to mass-produce babies regardless of the economic situation, economic postulations, economic advice or economic retardation of their regions or countries where they live in. The simple reason for the mass-baby making against the economic reality of their regions has always been based on their religion-faith rather than their survival reality. To people who live within the world where common-sense resides therefore, those who decide to commit humanitarian crime through mass-production of innocent children they can never be able to cater for are not innocent in the court of nature. However, after mass reproducing of these children, they do not stop there until they impact the kids with the fanatism of their religion without providing them any survival hope. Consequently, their regions/countries become volatile and hence, the need for migration and refuge-chaos" (Modupe, 2017).

Building on Modupe's argument above, it is very easy to draw certain conclusions from her analogy. The conclusion will include the fact that the explosively religionized population within those regions will eventually become viable for exportation to the targeted markets, which have always been the WESTERN/CHRISTIAN DOMINATED REGIONS IN THE NAME OF REFUGEES assistance. Whereas, the White or the innocent indigenes of these western countries scarcely give birth to children. At most, they beget one or two kids, which make the theory behind Modupe's analogy to become very realistic. And this is the fact as it is presenting itself, if the likes of President Trump is not coming up strong on immigration policies and/or coming into the Presidential authority in America. The circle of islamization may soon complete its tenure because such refugees with alien cultures, beliefs and religions who annually flock in their thousands will occupy and dominate the western territories in less than 20 more decades into the future. Everywhere will be islamized by that simple global strategy in just matter of years!

Citing a facebook post by one Mobarak Haidar, a renowned Pakistani Historian, after U.S. President Donald Trump recognized Jerusalem as the capital of Israel, on December 6, 2017, Mobarak (2017) stated:

"Muslims of The World... Have No Religious Basis to Rule Jerusalem.'
The Holy Koran spoke of Al-Aqsa Mosque when it was not a 'mosque'
in the Islamic sense. It was a holy place because of the prophets of
Israel, from Moses to Jesus. It was the holy spot of worship for Jews and
Christians. Obviously, there were no Muslims in the city of Jerusalem
till the era of Emir-ul-Momineen Umar ibn Khattab... The Prophet
[Muhammad] and his followers prayed with their faces toward this
Jewish-Christian holy temple because Kaaba (the present center of
Islamic Hajj) was full of idols."

Mobarak (2017) explained furthered that: "The Holy Koran spoke of
Al-Aqsa Mosque when it was not a 'mosque' in the Islamic sense. It
was a holy place because of the prophets of Israel, from Moses to Jesus.
It was the holy spot of worship for Jews and Christians. Obviously,
there were no Muslims in the city of Jerusalem till the era of Emir-
ul-Momineen Umar ibn Khattab... The Prophet [Muhammad] and
his followers prayed with their faces toward this Jewish-Christian holy
temple because Kaaba (the present center of Islamic Hajj) was full of
idols. After the 'Conquest of Mecca,' Muslims were told to turn their
faces toward Kaaba and away from Jerusalem. They have never faced
their loyalty toward Jerusalem after that, for the last 1,400 years. No
Muslim ever went to pray in Jerusalem till it was conquered by the
second caliph [Umar ibn Khattab], although there was no restriction
on Muslims. They do not go there today because it was no longer their
center. Christians were masters of Jerusalem before Muslims conquered
it. It is still a holy place for Christians. But Christians have no dispute
over ownership of the city. It is their religious right to visit the holy
city; and the Jews do not stop them. Muslims, too, should have the
same religious rights, and in fact they have those rights; Jews do not
stop them. Muslims of the world, therefore, have no religious basis
to rule Jerusalem. Most of the Muslims have never even wished to
visit Jerusalem. As for the political claim, only Palestinians can make
it and only they should negotiate. It cannot be a collective Muslim
claim. Quraishi Arabs were masters of Jerusalem for some time. Then
Mamluks, Muslim kings, took over. Turks came after them. Colonial
Christians were the last political rulers. It is interesting to note that
Iranian Muslims or Muslims of the Indian Subcontinent or Southeast
Asia or of Africa have never been its masters. They can claim only

spiritual ties. Active centers of Muslim faith are none other than the Holy Cities of Mecca and Medina. Iranians have never controlled these active centers. But they are passionately building deadly weapons and jihadi forces to conquer or destroy Israel. It is sectarian politics of hegemony which can generate nothing but division and pain."

From the conquest of Mecca to Medina, Islamic history has been one, which is none other than: 'infiltrate them and conquer them,' while their own territories are no go areas to other people who share different faith or belief. Like a popular placard displayed in recent years on social media about religious tolerance, the placard reads:

Picture 8.1.1: True Tolerance

Like it has often been said; there is a different between how things suppose to be and how it is. Religion is suppose to be peaceful and personal without undue encroachment into others' domain or attempts to usurp one's belief over the rest others. But unfortunately, among thousands of other religions that exist around the world (SEE APPENDIX 1, PAGES: 200 – 225), Islamic religion in particular has constantly declined rules and refused to play by the ethic of respect for others' religious views. While others may be restrained practicing their individual religion in many of their countries described as Islamic nations, such as Saudi Arabi, Iraq, Iran etc, the same Islamists get into other communities dominated or owned by other religious believers and practice Islam. In fact, they do not just come in to practice but they strive to establish Islamic Sharia laws in other people's backyards. This has been the culture. Islamic nations smartly tightened up their own territories against other religious and cultural infiltrations through their stringent regulations and Sharia laws. This is however not the major issue; the major issue is about their mission, practice and history of conquests.

From the history of migration, most of the cities dominated by Islamists today were previously owned by other people and cultures. But once those cities welcomed them with one hand, few decades after, even the two hands may no longer be sufficient to plead with them to thread gently in another man's land. They literally take over the territories and overpower the indigenes. To achieve the above is very easy for the sect because their strategies are located in their practices. Since some nominal Islamists of the 21st century may no longer find it easy or fanciful to declare Jihad on their host communities to be able to outrun them, however, they retain two key strategies to conquering, dominating or taking over other's territories. These two modern day key conquest-strategies are embedded in their factors of mass reproduction and loyalty to Islam through critical teachings and Islamization of their innocent younger generation. No matter the years of sojourner of a typical Islamist in a foreign land and despite the help and the assistance such foreign land may have accorded such a man, it is largely impossible for such a man to be loyal to the land that spoon-fed it. Rather, their primary loyalty has constantly been to their religion (There may be some exceptions to this rule but on the average, majority reflect this behavior). This has also been replicated possibly through the kind of messages that are being passed over to most of their offspring born right outside their home-land yet, this other generation still grows up with critical mindset against the host nations (or communities).

Still on the principle of true tolerance; it is crystal clear today that a typical foreigner especially one from different religious background cannot go into either of these major Arab or Islamic countries of Saudi Arabi, United Arab Emirate or Iraq today and give birth to children and expect to claim citizenship for those children by reasons of birth or up-bringing. Like the proverb goes, it may sometimes be easier for the camel to go through the hole of the needle than for such a thing to happen. The reality on ground is that there are enough laws, regulations and critical conditions that will naturally force those foreign-religious practitioners to take their children out of such lands if they want to eyes or push for such possibilities. However, as at the time of this write up, some religious historians have claimed that in the next few decades or centuries, some European countries previously dominated and founded by Christians or Jews and other religions may soon be declared as Islamic nations.

Countries on this list of speculations have included the Great Britain and France. In situation of the United Kingdom, today, the facts are obvious since half of England is now currently Arab dominated. Therefore, going by the simple logic of calculation, it is a fact that as long as the White and other indigenous English keep to their rate of child-birth which is an average of one or two kids; their Islamists counterparts have the higher advantage of taking over that land in near century. Politics (which is the way to governmental positions) is a game of number. This speculation is reaffirmed because the rate of reproduction in England between the White Indigenes and the Arab foreigners-turned citizens has been estimated on the ratio 1:3. This speaks volumes in itself that by another two to three more decades, "THE INDEGENES MAY BECOME THE MINORITY." And since democracy is still the way to power in that land, definitely, those numbers may speak for the foreigner-citizens on the day of elections. Hence, "THE ALIENS MAY RULE THEIR LANDS AND EVENTUALLY DICTATE TO THEM." In fact, by records, the English has already lost the control of its parliament to those who live among them.

In the case of France, the situation is critical. Statistically, the alien Islamists have outnumbered the real owner of France. According to statistics, out of every ten (10) birth rate per day in France, seven (7) are from Muslim family while only three (3) are from Christian homes. Kent (2008) buttressed this thus: "…Extremely low birth rates in most of Europe have fueled concerns about population decline, yet one segment of the continent's population—Muslims—continues to grow. The increasing number and visibility of Muslims in Western Europe, juxtaposed with the low fertility among non-Muslims, has led some Europeans to worry that the region will eventually have a Muslim majority, fundamentally changing Western European society."

Another writer also submitted that "Muslims are the fastest growing religious group in the world. The growth and regional migration of Muslims, combined with the ongoing impact of the Islamic State (also known as ISIS or ISIL) and other extremist groups that commit acts of violence in the name of Islam, have brought Muslims and the Islamic faith to the forefront of the political debate in many countries" (Michael, 2017).

To add to the foregoing, it has been clamored; most UN organizations are already Muslim-dominated and little wondered why the voting against Trump's Jerusalem declaration was overwhelming.

America remains the last country to possess. In America's situation however, if the rate of migration from the Arab world through refugee programs, which amount to hundred thousand (100,000) on yearly basis, has not been immediately interrupted by the government of Donald Trump, the great America may simply have ended up been sold out to his own strongest enemies called ISIS and Al'Qaedas in less than three to four more decades when the American-born Islamists eventually grow stronger to become the head of CIA and FBI. Howbeit, the collapse of the great America would have been messy and damaging to the rest of the world who attempt to hide under her strong opposition to terrorism.

And for purposes of reiteration, the victory of Donald J. Trump in the US national pool of 2016, over the popular or world-choice; is a spiritual one. The President of America himself knew this and he acknowledged it by his subsequent and open efforts to stick with the Evangelical group with whom he trusted in God every inch the way until he became a victor. Like the popular adage, the river that forgets its source may soon get dried up. This is why it is mostly believed that Donald Trump has decided to stick to the religious direction of his winning-team.

8.2   Trump's Proactiveness and the Chemical Weapon of North Korea's Kim Jong Un

President Barack Obama, the immediate past President of the United States, like other world leaders, had treated the situation in North Korea with less-seriousness unti the advent of Trump's presidency. This was so unfortunate because the man Kim Jong Un, whom they were trying to get diplomatic with kept abusing and crossing all the red-lines drawn by the world leaders in the past era. The more the leaders approached his situation through some sort of political processes, the more dreaded Kim Jong became in his push to improve and expand its nuclear activities.

According to a review on North Korea's nuclear activities in New York Times (2017) "The nuclear program can be traced back to about 1962, when North Korea committed itself to what it called 'all-fortressization,' which was the beginning of the hyper-militarized North Korea of today. In 1963, North Korea asked the Soviet Union for help in developing nuclear weapons, but was refused. The Soviet Union agreed to help North Korea develop a peaceful nuclear energy program, including the training of nuclear scientists. Later, China, after its nuclear tests, similarly rejected North Korean requests for help with developing nuclear weapons. Soviet engineers took part in the construction of the Yongbyon Nuclear Scientific Research Center and began construction of an IRT-2000 research reactor in 1963, which became operational in 1965 and was upgraded to 8 MW in 1974. In 1979 North Korea indigenously began to build in Yongbyon a second research reactor, an ore processing plant and a fuel rod fabrication plant. North Korea's nuclear weapons program dates back to the 1980s. Focusing on practical uses of nuclear energy and the completion of a nuclear weapon development system, North Korea began to operate facilities for uranium fabrication and conversion, and conducted high explosive detonation tests. In 1985 North Korea ratified the NPT but did not include the required safeguards agreement with the IAEA until 1992. In early 1993, while verifying North Korea's initial declaration, the IAEA concluded that there was strong evidence this declaration was incomplete. When North Korea refused the requested special inspection, the IAEA reported its noncompliance to the UN Security Council.

In 1993, North Korea announced its withdrawal from the NPT, but suspended that withdrawal before it took effect. Under the 1994 Agreed Framework, the U.S. government agreed to facilitate the supply of two light water reactors to North Korea in exchange for North Korean disarmament. Such reactors are considered 'more proliferation-resistant than North Korea's graphite-moderated reactors', but not 'proliferation proof.'"

The report furthered that: "Implementation of the Agreed Framework foundered, and in 2002 the Agreed Framework fell apart, with each side blaming the other for its failure. By 2002, Pakistan had admitted that North Korea had gained access to Pakistan's nuclear technology in the late 1990s. Based on evidence from Pakistan, Libya, and multiple confessions from North Korea itself, the United States accused North Korea of noncompliance and halted oil shipments; North Korea later claimed its public confession of guilt had been deliberately misconstrued. By the end of 2002, the Agreed Framework was officially abandoned. In 2003, North Korea again announced its withdrawal from the Nuclear Proliferation Treaty. In 2005, it admitted to having nuclear weapons but vowed to close the nuclear program. On October 9, 2006, North Korea announced it had successfully conducted its first nuclear test. An underground nuclear explosion was detected, its yield was estimated as less than a kiloton, and some radioactive output was detected. On January 6, 2007, the North Korean government further confirmed that it had nuclear weapons. On March 17, 2007, North Korea told delegates at international nuclear talks that it was preparing to shut down its main nuclear facility. The agreement was reached following a series of six party talks, involving North Korea, South Korea, China, Russia, Japan, and the United States begun in 2003.

According to the agreement, a list of its nuclear programs would be submitted and the nuclear facility would be disabled in exchange for fuel aid and normalization talks with the United States and Japan. This was delayed from April due to a dispute with the United States over Banco Delta Asia, but on July 14, International Atomic Energy Agency inspectors confirmed the shutdown of North Korea's Yongbyon nuclear reactor and consequently North Korea began to receive aid. This agreement fell apart in 2009, following a North Korean satellite launch. In April 2009, reports surfaced that North Korea has become a "fully fledged nuclear power", an opinion shared by International Atomic Energy Agency (IAEA) Director General Mohamed ElBaradei. On May 25, 2009, North Korea conducted a second nuclear test, resulting in an explosion estimated to be between 2 and 7 kilotons. The 2009 test, like the 2006 test, is believed to have occurred at Mantapsan, Kilju County, in the north-eastern part of North Korea. This was found by an earthquake occurring at the test site. In February 2012,

North Korea announced that it would suspend uranium enrichment at the Yongbyon Nuclear Scientific Research Center and not conduct any further tests of nuclear weapons while productive negotiations involving the United States continued. This agreement included a moratorium on long-range missiles tests. Additionally, North Korea agreed to allow IAEA inspectors to monitor operations at Yongbyon. The United States reaffirmed that it had no hostile intent toward the DPRK and was prepared to improve bilateral relationships, and agreed to ship humanitarian food aid to North Korea. The United States called the move 'important, if limited,' but said it would proceed cautiously and that talks would resume only after North Korea made steps toward fulfilling its promise" (New York Times, 2017).

However, it says, "after North Korea conducted a long-range missile test in April 2012, the United States decided not to proceed with the food aid. On February 11, 2013, the U.S. Geological Survey detected a magnitude 5.1 seismic disturbance, reported to be a third underground nuclear test. North Korea has officially reported it as a successful nuclear test with a lighter warhead that delivers more force than before, but has not revealed the exact yield. Multiple South Korean sources estimate the yield at 6–9 kilotons, while the German Federal Institute for Geosciences and Natural Resources estimates the yield at 40 kilotons. However, the German estimate has since been revised to a yield equivalent of 14 kt when they published their estimations in January 2016. On January 6, 2016 in Korea, the United States Geological Survey detected a magnitude 5.1 seismic disturbance, reported to be a fourth underground nuclear test. North Korea claimed that this test involved a hydrogen bomb. This claim has not been verified. As described below, a 'hydrogen bomb' could mean one of several degrees of weapon, ranging from enhanced fission devices to true thermonuclear weapons. Within hours, many nations and organizations had condemned the test. Expert U.S. analysts do not believe that a hydrogen bomb was detonated. Seismic data collected so far suggests a 6–9 kiloton yield and that magnitude is not consistent with the power that would be generated by a hydrogen bomb explosion. 'What we're speculating is they tried to do a boosted nuclear device, which is an atomic bomb that has a little bit of hydrogen, an isotope in it called tritium,' said

Joseph Cirincione, president of the global security firm Ploughshares Fund" (New York Times, 2017).

It continued that: "The German source which estimates for all the North Korea's past nuclear test has instead made an initial estimation of 14 kt, which is about the same (revised) yield as its previous nuclear test in 2013. However the yield estimation for January 2016 nuclear test was revised to 10 kt in the subsequent nuclear test from North Korea. On February 7, 2016, roughly a month after the alleged hydrogen bomb test, North Korea claimed to have put a satellite into orbit around the Earth. Japanese Prime Minister Shinzō Abe had warned the North to not launch the rocket, and if it did and the rocket violated Japanese territory, it would be shot down. Nevertheless, North Korea launched the rocket anyway, claiming the satellite was purely intended for peaceful, scientific purposes. Several nations, including the United States, Japan, and South Korea, have criticized the launch, and despite North Korean claims that the rocket was for peaceful purposes, it has been heavily criticized as an attempt to perform an ICBM test under the guise of a peaceful satellite launch. China also criticized the launch, however urged "the relevant parties" to "refrain from taking actions that may further escalate tensions on the Korean peninsula". A fifth nuclear test occurred on September 9, 2016. This test yield is considered the highest among all five tests thus far, surpassing its previous record in 2013. The South Korean government said that the yield was about 10 kt despite other sources suggesting a 20 to 30 kt yield. The same German source which has made estimation of all North Korea's previous nuclear tests suggested an estimation of a 25 kiloton yield. Other nations and the United Nations have responded to North Korea's ongoing missile and nuclear development with a variety of sanctions; on March 2, 2016, the UN Security Council voted to impose additional sanctions against North Korea. On February 18, 2017, China announced that it was suspending all imports of coal from North Korea as part of its effort to enact United Nations Security Council sanctions aimed at stopping the country's nuclear weapons and ballistic-missile program. On March 6, 2017, North Korea launched four ballistic missiles from the Tongchang-ri region towards the Sea of Japan. The launch was condemned by the United Nations as well as South Korea. The move prompted US Secretary of State Rex Tillerson to embark on a diplomatic mission ten days later to Japan, South Korea and China, in an effort to address the heightened international tension in the region. On April 13, 2017, White House representative Nick Rivero was quoted saying the United States was "very close" to engaging in some sort of retaliation towards North Korea. President Trump commented on North Korea by saying they will fight the war on terrorism no matter the cost. On April 15, 2017, at the yearly major public holiday also known in the country as the Day of the Sun, North Korea staged a massive military parade to commemorate the 105th birth anniversary of Kim Il-sung, the country's founder and grandfather of current leader, Kim Jong-un. The parade took place amid hot speculation in the United States, Japan, and South Korea that the country would also potentially test a sixth nuclear device, but failed to do so. The parade did show off, for the first time, two new intercontinental ballistic missile-sized canisters as well as submarine-launched ballistic missiles and a land-based version of the same. On April 16, 2017, hours after the military parade in Pyongyang, North Korea attempted to launch a ballistic missile from a site near the port of Sinpo, on the country's east coast. The missile exploded seconds after launch. Later that month, after a visit to Washington by the top Chinese leader, the US State Department announced that North Korea was likely to face economic sanctions from China if it conducted any further tests" (New York Times, 2017).

In addition, the report reveals that: "On April 28, 2017, North Korea launched an unidentified ballistic missile over the Pukchang airfield, in North Korean territory. It blew up shortly after take-off at approximately 70 kilometers (44 miles) altitude. On July 4, 2017, North Korea launched Hwasong-14 from Banghyon airfield, near Kusong, in a lofted trajectory it claims lasted 39 minutes for 578 miles (930 km), landing in the waters of the Japanese exclusive economic zone. US Pacific Command said the missile was aloft for 37 minutes, meaning that in a standard trajectory it could have reached all of Alaska, a distance of 4,160 miles (6,690 km). By targeting the deep waters in the Sea of Japan, North Korea was ensuring that American or Japanese divers would encounter difficulties when attempting to recover Hwasong 14's engine. Equally, North Korea was not attempting to recover any re-entry debris either, which South Korea pointed out is an indication that this first launch was of an ICBM which was far from ready for combat. As of July 2017, the U.S. estimated that North Korea would have a reliable nuclear-capable intercontinental ballistic missile (ICBM) by early 2018. On July 28, North Korea launched a second, apparently more advanced, ICBM, with altitude around 3,700 km, that traveled 1,000 km down range; analysts estimated that it was capable of reaching the continental United States. John Schilling estimates the current accuracy of the North's Hwasong-14 as poor, at the mooted ranges which threaten US cities. Michael Elleman points out that July 28, 2017 missile re-entry vehicle broke up on re-entry; further testing would be required. On August 8, 2017 *The Washington Post* reported that the Defense Intelligence Agency, in a confidential assessment, stated that North Korea has sufficiently miniaturized a nuclear warhead to fit inside one of its long-range missiles. On August 12 *The Diplomat* reported that the Central Intelligence Agency, in a confidential assessment from early August, has concluded that the reentry vehicle in the July 28 test of Hwasong-14 didn't survive atmospheric reentry due to apogee of 3,700 kilometers which caused structural stresses in excess of what an ICBM would have had in minimum energy trajectory. The CIA also concluded that North Korean reentry vehicle is likely advanced enough that it would likely survive reentry under normal minimum energy trajectory. On September 3, 2017, North Korea claimed to have successfully tested a thermonuclear bomb, also known as a hydrogen bomb. Corresponding seismic activity similar to an earthquake of magnitude 6.3 was reported by the USGS, making the blast around 10 times more powerful than previous detonations by the country. Later the bomb yield was estimated to be 250 kilotons, based on further study of the seismic data. The test was reported to be "a perfect success." Jane's Information Group estimates the explosive payload of the North Korean thermonuclear/hydrogen Teller-Ulam type bomb to weigh between 255 and 360 kilograms (562 and 794 lb)" (New York Times, 2017).

Going by the fore-going, it is clearly obvious that North Korea and its leadership have intended mission for their continuous focus on nuclear development while the rest of the world are thriving to build income and economy. If the Presidency of Donald J. Trump has not actively stepped into the shoe to lead the battle against the North Korea alongside other world leaders through the UN resolutions and America's deployment of war-artilleries, the world-leaders may have woken up in another decade only to discover that the world has produced another Adolf Hitler who may have carefully built enough nuclear capacity to subject every nation under its control. This may not be far from the agenda of North Korea under Kim Jong Un.

CHAPTER NINE

9.0 SKIN-COLOUR SUPREMACY–THE LIES OF SENTIMENT

Quote it or argue it, all over the world, people who are nice are nice; people who are mean are mean. It has nothing to do with their hair-color or the color of their skin. The issue of supremacy is more of human behavioral and attitudinal issue and has little or nothing to do with facial color. In other word, it is an individual factor rather than racial. This statement is fundamental to the position of this chapter of the book on the issue of skin-color supremacy-struggles; since some other school of thoughts have always enjoyed accusing certain race or people with certain skin-color of supremacy tendencies.

To be candid, any time the word supremacy is preceded by a prefix of skin-color such as "white-supremacy" as it is popularly clamoured; I feel so concerned for the dearth of knowledge exhibited by those who still embraced such sentimental opinion. For those who care to know what my reasons are, I have researched and I have found out that supremacy-factor in itself, is a problem of man. I wrote man, to mean all human with unregenerate mind. No doubt, there may have been some sort of skin-colour supremacy tendencies in decades before the current generation or dispensation, but the sincerity about supremacy issue lies more in the fact that it is a human factor. Every man has the tendency to dominate another. Every land-owner wants to suppress and oppress their tenants. Every rich man (whether black or yellow) wants to oppress the poor if he has his ways. Most people who 'Have' wants to dominate those who 'Do not have' based on whatever they have in their favor as advantage. Every man in position of authority has the potency of harassing those who are not in similar position. Every woman wants to dominate her man and, most men want to dominate their women etc. Hence, it is the right time we get it straight that supremacy is a man's problem, not racial.

From time immemorial; before the beginning of colonialism, students of history must have read that there were domineering and subjectivity practices, both in concaves and *'high-lands.'* There were oppressive activities within the remotest villages in European territories as well as in African suburbs. These oppressive activities were perpetrated by people of the same color and history and, against themselves. These barbaric practices of domination and oppression thrived among the different climes and people around the world. In fact, going by the epochs of societal development most ancient philosophers and theorists have established; it has been stated that after the dead of communal-living system of human relation, every other stage of human development has been ruled by one form of human supremacy-system or another. From the feudal system to the era of slavery and down to the modern day capitalist system of societal relation; it has been about one form of supremacy to another. The owner of means, the most successful hunters, the royal lineages as well as the successful entrepreneurers have always dominated and dictated to other common citizens in their climes. This is being said to mean 'intra-supremacy.' The external form of supremacy or dominance only came when colonialism era began.

Karl Marx, one of the earliest and popular philosophers wrote extensively on this subject-matter in his critical reviews on human-material relation. In Karl Marx's reflection on the subject-matter as contained in his historical materialism analysis; he referred to this issue as material conditions, which is "the relationships which people have with each other in order to fulfill basic needs such as feeding, clothing, and housing themselves and their families" (Marx, 1975). The need to fulfill these basic needs have always subjected one man under another. The capacity to provide these basic needs in sufficiency for one-self has always made some men to feel superior to others. This has nothing to do with age, race or colour. 'Blacks' have accommodated other 'blacks' and have oppressed and suppressed the ones being accommodated. This is also the same when you seek shelter in another nation other than where you are originally from; the human-factors in the providers of the shelters may at given time become inflated, which may result in the subject-matter of supremacy.

However, Marx enhanced our understanding of supremacy factor through the history of human development, going by his analysis of six successive stages of development. According to Marx, human development began from the primitive communism (called communalism), which was the only state in historical development that was devoid of supremacy. During this era, "there is no concept of ownership beyond individual possessions. The tribe shares everything in order to ensure its survival. Tribal societies have yet to develop large-scale agriculture and so their survival is a daily struggle. There is usually no concept of 'leadership' yet. So tribes are led by the best warrior if there is war, the best diplomat if they have steady contact with other tribes and so forth" (Marx, 1975). Marx (1975) further that, "the primitive communism stage most likely begins soon after the dawn of humanity itself." But since this historical stage of development ended as soon as men developed taste for private ownership of property, then the world has never been freed from the complications of supremacy. This is because the quest for private ownership gives rise to societal divisions. These divisions today have metamorphosed and have advanced above the primitive classification concept of "Human" versus "Other earthly materials" ("human" in this concept being every man or woman regardless of race, colour or geographical location, while "other earthly materials" mean other living & non-living things the mother earth avails man). Rather in today's world, we are now familiar with sibling's battle of supremacy due to the factor of who will own what. In some families, some elder brothers or younger brothers have been regarded to be more successful in their career or attainment, hence, they suddenly become superior to the rest siblings. It has degenerated into such situation where particular clans among the same generation of people feel better than the rest of the society; into community against community based on who preoccupied which lands first; into city against cities; into some nations feeling superior to some other nations since they possess better infrastructural capacity, industrial equipments or military-might than others. The situation has equally degenerated into the commonest 'racial (or skin-color) supremacy', where the world now erroneously focuses the light of attention. Whereas, on the micro levels, the world has recorded more suicide attempts when one successful man makes his brothers feel useless. The world has recorded more crimes, civil wars, jungle justices, over-night assailants among people of same color and nearness communities, due to factors of superiority indignations. Yet, most analysts still preoccupy their attention with the argument of skin-color superiority.

Marx's analysis of the rest five stages in historical development graphically depicted how the spirit of "I own" segregated a people among themselves into:

- The Slave class and the Ruling class era, which is popularly called: slave society. This was the next historical stage where "the private-property syndrome appears. Where there is always a slave-owning ruling class and the slaves themselves. Where democracy arises first with the development of the republican city-state, followed by the totalitarian empire in the history of man. Where citizens now own more than personal property. Land ownership becomes especially important during a time of agricultural development. Where the slave-owning class 'own' the land and slaves (these slaves being other human beings. And it is also important to note that this era cut across all races in human existence. Exhaustive African history revealed how wealthy black men and women as well as kings and queens made slaves of fellow ordinary poor black children before colonialism), which are the main means of producing wealth, whilst the vast majority of people have very little or nothing" (Marx, 1975).

- Feudalism emerged after the collapse of slave-age. According to Marx: "This was most obvious during the European Middle Ages when society moved from slavery to feudalism. It was an aristocracy form of government where the state was ruled by monarchs who inherit their positions, or at times marry or conquer their ways into leadership. Theocratically, this was a time of largely religious rule when there was only one religion in the land and its organizations affect all parts of daily life. Where castes can sometimes form and one's class is determined at birth with no form of advancement. Happenings in India made it more suitable as one of the good examples of regions where feudal practice was predominant. During feudalism there are many classes such as kings, lords, and serfs, some little more than slaves. Most of these inherit their titles for good or ill. At the same time that societies must create all these new classes, trade with other nation-states increases rapidly. This also catalyzes the creation of the merchant class, from whence a capitalist class emerges out of the merchants' riches, within this feudal society" (Marx, 1975).

- To Marx, special attention was paid to the capitalist stage of human historical/developmental evolvement because: "it was the one he lived on. In Marx's capitalism, the means of production are no longer in the hands of the monarchy and/or the nobility rather they are controlled by the bourgeois and the petit bourgeois classes. The bourgeoisie and the petit bourgeoisie control the means of production through commercial enterprises (such as corporations) which aim to maximize profit. In Marx's analysis, the bourgeoisie eventually (after years of struggle and opposition) accepted a form of democratic governance, descendent of the elective monarchy system (such as the Sejm of Poland-Lithuania) through elected representatives. Bourgeois democracy at its beginning had minimum wealth/status requirements and sometimes led to different weight in voting, depending on the wealth/status of the voter. Historically it has also excluded (by force, segregation, legislation or other means) sections of the population such as women, slaves, ex-slaves, ethnic, linguistic and religious minorities. Eventually the bourgeoisie accepted to extend the right to vote gradually to a large part of the population, although this did not necessarily lead to universal suffrage. A democratically elected government today usually only reaches power with heavy monetary support from the bourgeoisie, and even if it doesn't act directly on behalf of them, is forced to do so by the structure itself" (Marx, 1975). This is a supremacy arrangement, which is perpetrated all over the world today. As a factor of common knowledge, democratic government that exists within individual nation of the world exist among the same people of same color and for the same people of same color and by the same people of same color. Yet, it is a supremacy arrangement. This is the real concept of modern day supremacy, which the poor all over the world need to find a way around.

- Finally, Socialism and communism, the practice of these systems, have remained largely in the theory. They have been known more as propositions for future evolution. Only socialism has been attempted by few countries of the world and the collapsed of those systems have always been rapid.

Furthermore, in the modern generation where we all belong, news headlines have captured more horrible demonstrations of supremacy among people of same color than the traditional white against black issue, if truism will be allowed the chance to triumph over provincialism. In South Africa alone, more reportage of what could be regarded as advance and barbaric supremacism rent the airwave for several months unabated. This was a situation of brutal killings of other black men and women from other countries of Africa by black South-Africans in the name of "we don't want you in our country." What other demonstration of supremacy is above such inhuman brutality of other fellow black people? According to news stories:

"Prior to 1994, immigrants from elsewhere faced discrimination and even violence in South Africa. After majority rule in 1994, contrary to expectations, the incidence of xenophobia increased. ... In May 2008, a series of attacks left 62 people dead… The attacks were apparently motivated by xenophobia. In 2015, another nationwide spike in xenophobic attacks against immigrants in general prompted a number of foreign governments to begin repatriating their citizens. According to a 1998 Human Rights Watch report, immigrants from Malawi, Zimbabwe and Mozambique living in the Alexandra township were 'physically assaulted over a period of several weeks in January 1995, as armed gangs identified suspected undocumented migrants and marched them to the police station in an attempt to 'clean' the township of foreigners.' The campaign, known as 'Buyelekhaya' (go back home), blamed foreigners for crime, unemployment and sexual attacks. In September 1998 a Mozambican and two Senegalese were thrown out of a train. The assault was carried out by a group returning from a rally that blamed foreigners for unemployment, crime and spreading AIDS. In 2000 seven foreigners were killed on the Cape Flats over a five-week period in what police described as xenophobic murders possibly motivated by the fear that outsiders would claim property belonging to locals. In April 2015, there was an upsurge in xenophobic attacks throughout the country. The attacks started in Durban and spread to Johannesburg. Zulu King Goodwill Zwelithini has been accused of fuelling the attacks by saying that foreigners should 'go back to their countries.' In October 2015 there were sustained xenophobic attacks in Grahamstown in the Eastern Cape. It was reported more than 500 people were displaced and more than 300 shops and homes looted and, in some cases, destroyed altogether. Reports from the residents allege that the police's attitudes were that of indifference, with some participating in the looting. The policing of the attacks was elitist as there was a line on Beaufort street which pointed out where looting would be tolerated and where it would not be. Thus, looting was allowed in the township and not tolerated in town. The police only pacified the situation and restored order after a week of attacks and looting" *(Los Angeles Times, 2015)*.

Another modern day form of realistic demonstration of human wickedness and reckless acts of supremacy can be traced to recent activities in Libya. In Libya, it has taken the special interventions and instrumentations of international communities among which are the European and the American Whites to suppress activities of forceful slavery and dehumanization activities some black men meted out to their immigrant brothers from other African countries. According to a CNN report:

"there were sales of African migrants as slaves in the North African nation of Libya and these activities prompted protests in central Paris. It has also been strongly condemned by the African Union." Going by another CNN post investigative report which queried the rationale behind the existence of such slave-trade camps, the report revealed that the major reason is because: 'Libya is the main transit point for refugees and migrants trying to reach Europe by sea.' In each of the last three years, 150,000 people have made the dangerous crossing across the Mediterranean Sea from Libya. For four years in a row, 3,000 refugees have died while attempting the journey, according to figures from the International Organization for Migration (IOM), the U.N.'s migration agency. The Libyan Coast Guard — supported with funds and resources from the E.U. and more specifically, Italy — has cracked down on boats smuggling refugees and migrants to Europe. With estimates of 400,000 to almost one million people now bottled up Libya, detention centers are overrun and there are mounting reports of robbery, rape, and murder among migrants, according to a September, 2017 report by the U.N. human rights agency.

Conditions in the centers have been described as 'horrific,' and among other abuses, migrants are vulnerable to being sold off as laborers in slave auctions. 'It's a total extortion machine,' Lenard Doyle, Director of Media and Communications for the IOM in Geneva tells TIME. 'Fueled by the absolute rush of migrants through Libya thinking they can get out of poverty, following a dream that doesn't exist.' The IOM said in April that it had documented reports of 'slave markets' along the migrant routes in North Africa 'tormenting hundreds of young African men bound for Libya.' 'There they become commodities to be bought, sold and discarded when they have no more value," Doyle (2017) said.

Picture 9.1: Black selling blacks into slavery in Libya's slavery camp

Illegal immigrants are seen at a detention centre in Zawiyah, 45 kilometres west of the Libyan capital Tripoli, on June 17, 2017. Taha Jawashi—AFP/Getty Images (Source: http://time.com/5042560/libya-slave-trade/)

The modern day supremacy factor can further be cited in the relationship between the South and North Korean people who despite their close cultural and historical relations have been battling with the problem of supremacy for years, with the North trying to oppress, suppress and dominate its Southern counterpart. As reviewed on Wikipedia (2018):

"The list of attacks include: engagements on land, air, and sea, but does not include alleged incursions and terrorist incidents that occurred away from the border. A total of 3,693 armed North Korean agents have infiltrated into South Korea between 1954 and 1992, with 20% of these occurring between 1967 and 1968. Many of the incidents occurring at sea are due to border disputes. In 1977 North Korea claimed an Exclusive Economic Zone over a large area south of the disputed western maritime border, the Northern Limit Line in the Yellow Sea. This is a prime fishing area, particularly for crabs, and clashes commonly occur, which have been dubbed the 'Crab Wars.' As of January 2011, North Korea had violated the armistice 221 times, including 26 military attacks. Also on 16 February 1958: North Korean agents hijack a South Korean airliner to Pyongyang en route from Busan to Seoul; 1 American pilot, 1 American passenger, 2 West German passengers, and 24 other passengers were released in early March, but 8 other passengers remained in the North. In 1964 equally, North Korea creates an underground group: Revolutionary Party for Reunification, this group is ground down and eliminated by South Korean authorities by 1969. On January 17, 1968: In an incident known as the Blue House Raid, a 31-man detachment from the Korean People's Army secretly crosses the DMZ on a mission to kill South Korean President Park Chung-hee on January 21, nearly succeeding. The incursion was discovered after South Korean civilians confronted the North Koreans and informed the authorities. After entering Seoul disguised as South Korean soldiers, the North Koreans attempt to enter the Blue House (the official residence of the President of South Korea). The North Koreans are confronted by South Korean police and a firefight ensued. The North Koreans fled Seoul and individually attempted to cross the DMZ back to North Korea. Of the original group of 31 North Koreans, 28 were killed, one was captured, and two are unaccounted for."

Additionally, the report stated: "26 South Koreans were killed and 66 were wounded, the majority of whom were soldiers and police officers. Three American soldiers were also killed and three were wounded. And happenings in recent years, have also recorded major cross fire exchanges like the one in January 27, 2010, where North Korea fires artillery shells into the water near Baengnyeong Island and South Korean vessels return fire. Three days later, North Korea continued to fire artillery towards the area. In October 10, 2014: North Korean forces fire anti-aircraft rounds at propaganda balloons launched from Paju. South Korean military return fire after a warning. While another one was witnessed on October 19, 2014: A group of North Korean soldiers approach the South Korean border and South Korean soldiers fired warning shots. The North Korean soldiers return fire before retreating. No injuries or property damage result. On January 3, 2016: South Korean soldiers fired warning shots at a suspected North Korean drone near the DMZ. While on December 21, 2017: a North Korean soldier crossed the DMZ to defect to South Korea. 40 minutes later shots were fired at the North Korean side of the DMZ, though the defector was not fired upon amidst the rest list of attacks and counter attacks between two supposedly neighboring-sister countries with same skin color and racial history" (Wikipedia 2018).

In all honesty to truism, historical documentations have never exonerated other Whites from the fury of Adolf Hitler's war of supremacy against the world during the world wars. The entire world inhabitants were meant to be the subjects in Hitler's conquest plans. He did not exonerate the White from other European countries or America in his proposed dominance of human race before the collapse of his campaign. This equally goes a long way to buttress the fact that the issue of supremacy is a problem beyond the sentiment of skin-colors as it is used today to distract attention from the real oppressors; to distract the poor from recognizing that those who plundered them are among them.

What also learnt credence to this disposition is the problem of human trafficking around the world today. The pattern of operation and the domain of activities have also established the fact that both the traffickers and the victims are usually people of same colors and, they are mostly country men and women of the same nationalities. This therefore keeps one to wonder why the noise has be predominantly more about racial supremacy rather than intra-supremacies and symptoms of wickedness that are being perpetrated and demonstrated around the world between people of same colors and, with shared history.

CHAPTER TEN

10.0 IN AN ELITIST-WORLD, THE POOR ARE THE PROBLEM OF THEMSELVES: SOCIAL STRATIFICATION AND THE UPPER CLASS DOMINANCE IN AMERICA POLITICS.

From time immemorial, societies have been class driven. The slave owners and the slaves; the nobles and the peasants; the land-owners and the serfs among other outdated societal structures that have existed through epochs. In a capitalist society which America champions, there exist the ruling class and the ruled; the bourgeoisie and the proletariats. Basically, social stratification is a form of inequality that occurs due to the inherent differences between human beings and this can be determined by race, gender, age, and economic capacity among other distinguishing features. The differentiation is done to mark one group as superior over another which leads to social classes arranged as hierarchies. According to Karl Marx, the capitalist mode of production consists of two main economic parts: the substructure and the Superstructure. Marx believes that stratification in capitalist society is predicated upon the idea of those who have wealth controlling or subjugating those who lack it.

The capitalist nation of America is an Elite dominance state which parades elites such as: political elites, economic elites and religion elites. Over decades, the political elites in America have been in control of American politics, calling the shots regarding who comes and goes out of power, while the economic elites were merely confined to economic and resource related activities. At worse, the economic elites have always assisted or supported the political elites to attain power and this has been the status-quo. However, with the recent victory of a business mogul, Mr. Donald Trump (an economic elite), against the caucus-interest of the Republican GOP (the political elites) in the party primary elections; the status-quo of the power-monopolized political caucus (elites) within the Republican Party was challenged and thwarted. The voters for reasons best known to them chose to elect one of the caste class/personality. This is unique in the sense that the lower class or the populace that need to carefully consider their choice or interest along certain known political criteria did not toe that line but rather focused on the economic and personal achievements of the candidate as against demands for his political reputation or caucus approval. Much as this deviant behavior of the masses-voters demonstrated to the establishment (the political class) that the real power belongs to the people; it remains a conundrum if the same masses can be able to repeat this kind of gesture to voting into power one day, one poor-man amidst themselves.

Wealth and education however, have been recognized as most common indexes of personal achievement. College education is also an important dimension in social stratification especially with the treat to college ranking in America which makes some colleges or universities create a class of theirs with ego of superiority against the general others. This college grading equally pulls weight in favor of the elitist class since people treat this class of educated elites better and accord them preferences while such preferential treatments also lead to wealth acquisition later in life. This known fact was reflective, studying through Mr. Donald Trump's sudden developmental antecedents in politics and/or in his campaign movements. Additionally, his display of wealth and flamboyant lifestyle got him more attention in both national and international media. This invariably created more focus on him among the populace and more historically, within the republican voters. His popularity grew in turns of victories such that his rooted politician-opponents had to give up the candidacy race for him to emerge as the presumptive nominee after their turns of disappointing political calculations in the 2016 Republican Party's primaries.

According to submissions from the numerous media analyses that stormed the airwaves after his astonishing performance in the

Republican Party primaries in 2016; Trump was adjudged to be 'popularity right' but 'politically incorrect.' Since political flag bearers of any party all over the world are usually chosen base on their pledge to party manifestoes, respect for party leadership and evidence of political experience through commensurate political growth over time. For instance, it was expected of him to have risen through the rank of a governor or senator before he could savor the interest of vying for such prestigious office of President of the United State through any of the two major political parties. This was the political traditions before any prospecting individual or candidate could be considered to have measured up and if such candidate had hoped to make any meaningful impact at the poll ordinarily. This self/traditional qualification procedure is appraised for purposes of accountability and track records, since most American Presidents are known for their good public service records before coming into office, as against the nomination of a non-bureaucratic business mogul whose flamboyant lifestyle may clearly negate an attribute befitting that of someone occupying the number one position of the most populous country in the world. The critical leadership roles an American president has to play among other prominent other countries of the world leant credence to this. Without isles of permutation, there is clearly a shift in the political paradigm as a result of whatever theory of revolution that gravitated Mr. Trump's victories at both primaries and general elections in 2016.

Poverty aside gender has however remained one of the major variables in societal stratification. According to World Health Organization reports (2010), a staggering number of Americans currently live below the poverty level. Seeing poverty as it is; it has been termed to relate more with lacks and, it is an exceptionally complicated social phenomenon in definition, cause and, its effects cannot actually be effectively gauged. Some theorists have accused the poor of being responsible for their poverty while others characterized them as fatalists or as those who have resigned themselves to fate or to a situation in which nothing can be done to change their economic predicament. Though, this can only be deemed to be correct due to the way some poor people actually see themselves. Nevertheless, some other theorists such as the proponents of deficiency theory have opined differently that social conditions trap individuals and groups into poverty and not really that they are the ones interested in being poor. In fact, the critics of innate inferiority and culture-of-poverty theory's explanations submitted that, before blaming the victim of poverty, the class system within the society must equally be critically looked into. Since the source of the problem may lie not in the victims, but in the way the society is organized around the advantage of 'a few-some' to the disadvantage of 'the majority-others.' Exploring this argument further may lead one to aligning with the view of R.K Merton on his theory of deviance which talks about the societal goals and the means to achieving them, especially more, given the background of an uneven social class within a capitalist state.

The poor therefore need to wake up to the awareness and the reality that the power actually belong to them as voters and electorates and, they should be willing/organized to redefine a class of their own to put the poor with similar socio-economic disadvantage like them in power, otherwise, the elite class may keep things as it is and continuously widened the dominance gap between the two classes that exist within the society. This was where the average American citizens in the lower class or the working class got things wrong in 2016 like their decision has always been several other many years in the past. Clearly, the two political parties that offered the electorates the choice of whom to elect in that year only provided the society with two different personalities from both the economic and political sections of the societal elites or caucuses. The poor were never represented and they have never been represented. The chance of the ordinary peasant-son in getting to the position of power kept dwindling by the years, yet, the postulation remains that, "the power belongs to the masses."

What then are these masses doing with the power in their hands? This power needs to be transformed into having adequate representatives constantly and practically at corridors of powers? According to a political misconception, if a rich candidate wins the seat of power, he/she will redraw the poverty line in favor of the poor, but the proponents of this postulation forgot that what has always prolonged the class-society in history has remained the ability of the upper class to customize the positions of power to themselves and consequently keep the poor where they belong. If the poor will not get proactive and redefined their social relation to the positions of power therefore, by rallying round candidate(s) from among them against the dictates of the upper class, they may continue to be used as mere 'TOOLS' in the Upper-class' quest for power. Hence, the poor has the power to save itself and redefine the societal arrangement towards power acquisition in an egalitarian society, within which the United States take the lead.

For instance, if the pendulum of 2016 elections had swung the other way round and Hilllary Clinton had emerged as the President; the poor still got nothing much to gain because she was also a highly rated member of a political elite class. In fact, she was a former first lady, which meant she was a perfect example of how the political elites launched-out towards recycling themselves around the seats of power.

The process is and it has always been an all exclusive reserve of the UPPER CLASS within the American society. Nevertheless, to thwart this age-long societal arrangement towards power acquisition, the poor (the lower and the middle classes) needs to regroup and redefined a class of their own (either in the name of labor movement or the Peasant's Party) and, subsequently muster their supports for the ones from among them. Otherwise, American society, like many others around the world, shall remain structuralized in favor of the upper class or elitist political domination.

REFERENCES

Andrew, S. (2017). Trump's Ta reform to save $4000 indebtedness. https://www.usnews.com/news/ economy/articles/2017-10-11/ trump-typical-household-to-save-4-000-with-tax-reform. retrieved: 01/26/2018.

Anthony, M. (2008). "Impeach Bush, Wexler says". South Florida Sun-Sentinel.com. https://en.wikipedia.org/wiki/Efforts_to_impeach_George_W._Bush. Retrieved: 01/16/2018

Appelbaum, R. P., and Chambliss, W. J. (1997). Sociology. Texas: Longman Pub Group.

BBC News (2017). US expands travel ban to include N Korea. http:// Mr Trump's original.ban-was_highly controversial, as it affected six majority-Muslim countries, and was widely _labeled-a-Muslim ban. Retrieved: 01/14/2018.

Bier, D. (2017). "Court Rules the President Violated the 1965 Law with Executive Order". Cato Institute. https://en.wikipedia.org/wiki/Executive_Order_13769 .
Retrieved: 01/10/2018.

Brewer, H. (1997). "Entailing Aristocracy in Colonial Virginia: 'Ancient Feudal Restraints' and Revolutionary Reform". William and Mary Quarterly. 54 (2): 307–46. https://en.wikipedia.org/wiki/Thomas_Jefferson.
Retrieved: 01/09/2018.

Brinkley, A. (2009). American History: A Survey. New York: McGraw-Hill. Vol. II., p. 887.

CBS News, (2017). https://www.cbsnews.com/ pictures/ presidents-ranked-from-worst-to-best-presidential-historians-survey-2017/40/. Retrieved: 01/04/2018.

Cengage, A. (2012). Liberty, Equality, Power: A History of the American People. https://en.wikipedia.org/wiki/ Ulysses_S._Grant_presidential_administration_scandals.
Retrieved: 01/07/2018.

Charles, F. W. & Tomas, F. (2007). "Religiousness and Fertility Among European Muslims," *Population and Development Review* 33, No. 4: 785-809

CNN News Story, 2017 "Slave trade photos in Libya" <img src="https:// timedotcom. files.wordpress.com/2017/12/gettyimages-696975984.jpg" alt="Illegal immigrants are seen at a detention centre in Zawiyah, 45 kilometres west of the Libyan capital Tripoli, on June 17, 2017."> Retrieved: 01/10/2018.

Congress.gov. (2015). "H.R.158 – Visa Waiver Program Improvement and Terrorist Travel Prevention Act of 2015".

Congressional Budget Office (2007). "The Impact of Unauthorized Immigrants on the Budgets of State and Local Governments." The Congress of the United States .

Conyers, J. (2005). "Creating a select committee to investigate the Administration's intent to go to war before congressional authorization, manipulation of pre-war intelligence, encouraging and countenancing torture" New York: Junior Publishers.

Connon M. (2017). "Immigration policies and World issues." Toronto: Strugfords Publishers.

Crapol, E. P. (2006). John Tyler, the Accidental President. North Carolina: University of North Carolina Press. https://en.wikipedia. org/wiki/John_Tyler. Retrieved: 01/06/2018.

Devine, M. J. (2009). The State of Israel, and the Quest for Peace in the Middle East. Truman: Truman State University Press. p. 93. https://en.wikipedia.org/wiki/Harry_S._Truman. Retrieved: 01/20/2018.

Diamond, J. & Almasy, S. (2017). "Trump's immigration ban sends shockwaves". CNN. https://en.wikipedia.org/ wiki/Executive_ Order_13769. Retrieved: 01/20/2018.

Djajić, S. (1997). "Illegal Immigration and Resource Allocation". *International Economic Review.* **38** (1).

Duke, E. (2017). "Memorandum on Rescission Of Deferred Action For Childhood Arrivals (DACA)". *United States Department of Homeland Security.*

Dusinberre, W. (2002). "President Polk and the Politics of Slavery." American Nineteenth Century History 1–16. https:// ipfs.io/ipfs/QmXoypizjW3WknFiJnKLwHCnL72vedxj QkDDP1mXWo6uco/wiki/James_K._Polk.html. Retrieved: 01/23/2018.

Edel, C. N. (2014). "Nation Builder: John Quincy Adams and the Grand Strategy of the Republic." Harvard Univ. Press https:// en.wikipedia.org/wiki/Presidency_of_John_Quincy_Adams. Retrieved: 01/10/2018.

Eitzen, D. S. and Maxine B. (1994). Social Problems. (6rd Ed.) Boston: Allyn and Bacon

Eliot A. C. (2017). Trump and the New American Era. https://www. theatlantic.com/magazine/archive/2017/10/ is-trump-ending-the-american-era/537888/. Retrieved: 01/02/2018.

Elspeth S. (2011). "A History of Donald Trump's Net Worth Publicity (1988–2011)". *http://dyp.sutd_srcsjfdsk/. Retrieved:* 01/09/2018.

Executive Order 13769 (2017). Protecting the Nation From Foreign Terrorist Entry Into the United States. Executive Office of the President. 82 FR 8977–8982. February 1, 2017.

Frank, F.& Hugh, S.(2006). "The Presidents of the United States of America," Washington D.C.: White House Historical Association. https://www.whitehouse.gov/about-the-white-house/presidents/ andrew-jackson/. Retrieved: 01/09/2018.

Fred I. G. (2002).n History of the United States. http://www. encyclopedia.com/people/history/us-history-biographies/dwight-david-eisenhower. Retrieved: 01/02/2018.

Frum, D. (2000). *How We Got Here: The '70s. New York. New York: Basic Books. pp. xxiii, 301.* (https://en.wikipedia.org/wiki/Presidency_of_Gerald_Ford *Retrieved: 01/01/2018*

Gage, B. (2008). "Our First Black President?". The New York Times. https://en.wikipedia.org/wiki/Warren_G._Harding. Retrieved: 01/07/2018.

Gasaway, J. G. (1999). Tippecanoe and the Party Press Too: Mass Communication, Politics, Culture, and the Fabled Presidential Election of 1840 (Thesis). Champaign/Urbana, Illinois: University of Illinois: https://en.wikipedia.org/wiki/William_Henry_Harrison_pr esidential_campaign,_1840. Retrieved: 01/08/2018.

Greg, R. (2009). A Tragedy of Democracy: Japanese Confinement in North America. mhttp://www.encyclopedia.com/ people/history/us-history-biographies/dwight-david-eisenhower. Retrieved: 01/04/2018.

Griswold, D. T. (2012). *"Immigration and the Welfare State". Cato Journal. 32 (1).*

Guardian News Papers (2017). What is D A C A ? https://www.theguardian.com/us news/2017/sep/04/donald-trump-what-is-daca-dreamers. Retrieved: 01/22/2018.

Harrington, M. (1984). The New American Poverty. New York: Holt, Rinehart, and Winston.

Harvey, G. (2000). *Indigenous Religions: A Companion.* (Ed: Graham Harvey). London and New York: Cassell. Page 06.

Hawks, L. (2012). The Government of Potus James Madison. https://llbah.wordpress.com/government/19th-century/4th-potus-james-madison-1809-1817-dem-rep/. Retrieved: 01/12/2018.

Henslin M. J. (1999). Sociology: A down-to-earth approach. USA, Nineth Edition. World Health Organization Report, 2008.

Herbert, S. P. & Marie, B. H. (2013). *Never Again: A President Runs for a Third Term* (1968) ed. Richard B. and Allan J. , *FDR and the*

Jews. https://en.wikipedia.org/ wiki/Criticism_of_Franklin_D._ Roosevelt. Retrieved: 01/18/2018.

Hirschfeld, D. J. (2015) "Mount McKinley Will Be Renamed Denali". The New York Times.

History on the Net (2012). https://www.historyonthenet.com/ authentichistory/1865-1897/3-gilded/6-cleveland2/index.html. Retrieved: 01/17/2018.

Houghton, M. H. (2010). Webster's New World College Dictionary (2010). "Deviation" 4th Edition. https://www.collinsdictionary. com/us/dictionary/english/ deviation. Retrieved: 01/08/2018.

James, B.L. (2017). The scary statistic that shows why Trump needs to fix Social Security now. https://www.cnbc.com/2017/03/28/ scary-social-security-statistic-commentary.html. Retrieved: 01/26/2018.

James C. (2006) "Time and Chance" https://www.npr.org/templates/ story/story.php?storyId= 6685816. Retrieved: 01/17/2018.

James, M. (2017). : Domestic Affairs". Miller Center of Public Affairs, University of Virginia. https://en.wikipedia.org/wiki/Presidency_of_ James_Monr oe. Retrieved: 01/12/2018.

Johnson, H. (2003). Sleepwalking Through History: America in the Reagan Years. New York: W. W. Norton & Co. Inc., p. 184.

Jonathan, T. (2017). President Trump and Barack Obama Undermined Lawyer Arguments: Opinion columnist. https://www.usatoday. com/story/opinion/2017/09/06/da ca-president-trump-and- barack-obama-undermine-lawyers-arguments-all-sides-jonathan- turley-column/637094001/. Retrieved: 01/22/2018.

Keith T. P. (2016). "What Does Immigration Actually Cost Us?" The New York Times. https://www.nytimes.com/2016/09/29/ opinion/campaign-stops/what-does-immigration-actually-cost- us.html. Retrieved: m 01/06/2018.

Kent, M. M. (2008). Muslims In Europe. http://www.prb.org/ Publications/Articles/2008/muslimsin europe.aspx. Retrieved: 01/03/2018.

Kopan, T. (2017). *"Trump ends DACA, but gives Congress window to save it". CNN.* https://en.wikipedia.org/ wiki/Deferred_Action_ for_Childhood_Arrivals. Retrieved: 01/12/2018.

Lacroix, P. (2016). "Choosing Peace and Order: National Security and Sovereignty in a North American Borderland, 1837– 42". The International History. https://en.wikipedia.org/wiki/Presidency_ of_Martin_Van_ Buren. Retrieved: 01/11/2018.

Lavender, P. (2015). *"Jimmy Carter Blasts U.S. 'Political Bribery'".* New York: Huffington Post. https://en.wikipedia.org/ wiki/Jimmy_ Carter. Retrieved: 01/18/2018

LawLogix. H. (2013). "What is the DREAM Act and who are DREAMers?" https://en.wikipedia.org/wiki/ Deferred_Action_ for_Childhood_Arrivals

Lenard, D. (2018). "Libya Slave Trade" Director of Media and Communications for the IOM in Geneva. http://time. *com/5042560/libya-slave-trade/. Retrieved: 01/15/2018.*

Liu, X. (2010). *"Labor Market Search and the Dynamic Effects of Immigration". Journal of Economic Dynamics and Control. 12 (34).*

Loftus, D. (2016) *"Rutherford B. Hayes's visit to Oregon, 1880". The Oregon Encyclopedia.* https://en.wikipedia.org/ wiki/Rutherford_B._ Hayes. Retrieved: 01/09/2018.

Los Angeles Times (2018), "Woodrow Wilson: World Statesman" by Kendrick A. Clements, Professor of history, South Carolina University. http://www.latimes.com/opinion/la-oe-catania18-2009jan18-story.html. Retrieved: 01/05/2018.

Los Angeles Times (2015). "Attacks on foreigners spread in South Africa; weekend violence feared". https://en.wikipedia.org/ wiki/ Xenophobia_in_South_Africa. Retrieved 01/11/ 2018.

Los Angeles Times, (2018). "Abraham Lincoln: Redeemer President" by Allen Guelzo, a Professor of history and Civil War-era studies, Gettysburg College.: http://www.latimes.com/opinion/la-oe-catania18-2009jan18-story.html. Retrieved: 01/12/2018.

Macomber, D. (2016). One Simple Act. Discovering the Power of Generosity. New York: Howard Books. p. 83.

Matthews, D. (2016). "The sexual harassment allegations against Bill Clinton, explained". https://en.wikipedia.org/wiki/ Bill_Clinton_ sexual_misconduct_allegations. Retrieved: 01/15/2018.

Michael, L. (2017). Muslims and Islam: Key findings in the U.S. and around the world. http://www.pewresearch.org/fact-tank/2017/08/09/muslims-and-islam-key-findings-in-the-u-s-and-around-the-world/. Retrieved: 01/09/2018.

Michal, K. (2017). "Past Presidents Affairs" http://www.businessinsider. com/author/michal-kran. Retrieved: 01/11/2018.

Migration Policy Institute (2015). "Ten Facts About U.S. Refugee Resettlement." By Randy C. and Michael F. https://www.migrationpolicy.org/research/ten-facts-about-us-refugee-resettlement?gclid=EAIaIQobChMIw8 Ce0Mz42AIVxrrACh2hmQWnEAA YASAAEgJOi_D_BwE. Retrieved: 01/09/2018.

Mobarak, H. (2017). Jerusalem, Declaration. https://www.facebook. com/mobarak.haider. Retrieved: 01/02/2018.

Modupe, O. (2017) "Views on Religions and Islamization" Ibadan: Bedslab Publishers.

Moy, H.M. (2006). "The simple analytics of optimal growth with illegal migrants: A clarification". Journal of Economic Dynamics and Control. 30 (12): 2469–2475.

National Academies of Engineering Medicine (2016) "Immigration, Panel on the Economic and Fiscal Consequences of Statistics, Committee on National; Education." Division of Behavioral and Social Sciences and; Sciences. http://The Economic and Fiscal Consequences of Immigration. doi:10.17226/23550.Retrieved: 01/09/2018.

New York Times (2017). The Key Spending Cuts and Increases in Trump's Budget. https://www.nytimes.com/2017/ 05/22/ us/politics/trump-budget-winners-losers.html. Retrieved: 01/21/2018.

New York Times (2017). " North Korea and the Threat of Chemical Warfare." By Theo E. https://www.nytimes.com/ 2017/10/27/ opinion/north-korean-chemical-weapons.html. Retrieved: 01/12/2018

Newby, J. (2012). "Publisher's 1991 booklet says Barack Obama 'was born in Kenya'". Examiner.com website/News/Politics/ Republican.

Norton & Company (2018). American Foreign Policies. http://www. wwnorton.com/college/polisci/american-foreign-policy4/ch/01/ review.aspx. Retrieved: 01/21/2018.

O'Brien, T. L. (2005). "What's He Really Worth?" The New York Times.

Osmanski, S. (2017). Who Is the Mother of Donald Trump, Jr.? Everything You Need to Know About Donald Trump's Ex-Wife, Ivana Trump! http://www.closerweekly.com/posts/who-is-donald-trump-jr-mother-136509. Retrieved: 01/20/2018.

*Palivos, T. & Yip, C. (2010). "Illegal immigration in a heterogeneous labor market". Journal of Economics. **101** (1): 21–47.*

*Palivos, T. (2009). "Welfare Effects of Illegal Immigration". Journal of Population Economics. **22** (1).*

Panetta, A. (2015). "Donald Trump's grandfather ran Canadian brothel during gold rush". CBC News.

Pew Research Center (2017). "5 facts about illegal immigration in the U.S."http://_5_facts_illegal-immigration-the-US/_current. Retrieved: 01/08/2018.

Pollak, J. B. (2012). "The vetting—exclusive—Obama's literary agent in 1991 booklet: 'Born in Kenya and raised in Indonesia and Hawaii'". Breitbart website/Big government. Breitbart. com. http://www.conservapedia.com/ Barack_Hussein_Obama. Retrieved: 01/19/2018.

Pruitt, S. (2016). "10 Things You Might Not Know About Lyndon B. Johnson" http://www.history.com/news/history-lists/10-things-you-might-not-know-about-lyndon-b-johnson. Retrieved: 01/03/2018.

Reitwiesner, W. A. (2016). "The Ancestors of Senator John Forbes Kerry." http://www.wargs.com/political/ kerry.html.Retrieved: 01/12/2018.

Relman, E. (2017). "Sexual Assault Allegations against Clinton." http://www.businessinsider.com/ these-are-the-sexual-assault-allegations-against-bill-clinton-2017-11/#juanita-broaddrick-1Marx, *Preface to A Contribution to the Critique of Political Economy Marx, Early writings*, Penguin, 1975, p425-6

Richard, G. (2017). Things You Should Know About DACA. https://www.npr.org/2017/09/05/548754723/5-things-you-should-know-about-daca. Retrieved: 01/09/2018.

Robert, S. (2016). "World Politics in International Migration." England: Oxford Press. Pp. 123 -129.

Roberts, G. B. (1995). Ancestors of American Presidents. New England: Historic Genealogical Society. p. 199 https://www.cbsnews.com/ pictures/presidents-ranked-from-worst-to-best-presidential-historians-survey-2017/18/. Retrieved: 01/06/2018.

Rozhon, T. (2017). "Fred C. Trump, Postwar Master Builder of Housing for Middle Class, Dies at 93". The New York Times. https://en.wikipedia. org/wiki/Donald_Trump. Retrieved: 01/20/2018.

Sean, K.. (2017). Toughest Countries to get into around the World. http://www.bootsnall.com/articles/12-10/top-10-toughest-countries-to-get-into.html. Retrieved: 01/20/2018.

Shapiro, B.(2012). "Obama's lit agency used 'born in Kenya' bio until 2007". Breitbart website/Big government. Breitbart.com. http://www.conservapedia.com/ Barack_Hussein_Obama. Retrieved: 01/19/2018

Solomont, E. (2015). "A Piece of History Stands Hidden on Brooklyn Bridge". The New York Sun. https://en.wikipedia.org/wiki/Presidency_of_George_Was hington. Retrieved: 01/02/2018.

Stump, S. (2016). "Donald Trump: My dad gave me 'a small loan' of $1 million to get started". CNBC. https://en.wikipedia.org/wiki/Donald_Trump . Retrieved: 01/22/2018.

Tolson, J (2007) The Presidency of James Buchanan. https://en.wikipedia.org/wiki/Presidency_of_James_Buch anan. Retrieved: 01/13/2018.

Tolson, J. (2007). Reports on the Worse Presidents of America. https://www.usnews.com/news/special-reports/the-worst-presidents/articles/2014/12/17/worst-presidents-herbert-hoover-1929-1933. Retrieved: 01/02/2018.

Tom, O. (2017). Trump and Syria Bombing. http://www.newsweek.com/trump-war-bombing-syria-challenge-russia-iran-629526. Retrieved: 01/18/2018.

Trump, D. (2017) "Travel Ban" https://www.mirror.co.uk/news/world-news/donald-trumps-muslim-ban-reversed-9756660. Retrieved: 01/08/2018.

U.S News, (2014). Special Report on the worse Presidents of America. https://www.usnews.com/news/special-reports/the-worst-presidents/articles/2014/12/17/worst-presidents-andrew-johnson-1865-1869. Retrieved: 01/10/2018.

U.S. Department of State (2017). "Report of the Visa Office 2016". Bureau of Consular Affairs. http://travel.state.gov/. *Retrieved: 01/12/2018.*

United States Department of Homeland Security (2017). "Visa Waiver Program Improvement and Terrorist Travel Prevention Act Frequently Asked Questions". U.S. Customs and Border Protection.

University of Virginia (2017). "Past Presidents of America. https://millercenter.org/president/john-f-kennedy/key-events. Retrieved: 01/02/2018.

Vergote, A., (1997) *Religion, belief and unbelief:* a psychological study, Leuven University Press. p. 89 Webster (2010). "Biographies and Encyclopedias of Reference." Poland: Ziporraph Ltd.

White, M. (2016), Ulysses S. Grant presidential administration scandals. https://en.wikipedia.org/wiki/Ulysses_S._Grant. Retrieved: 01/20/2018.

Wikipedia (2018): "North Korea and south Korea issues." http://hostility_between.North.Korea_Versu_South.Korea_. Retrieved: 01/04/2018.

Wikipedia, (2018). "List of Border Incidents Involving North and South Korea" https://en.wikipedia.org/ wiki/List_of_border_incidents_involving_North_and_Sout h_Korea. Retrieved: 01/15/2018.

Wood, G. S. (2009). Empire of Liberty: A history of the Early Republic, 1789–1815. New Yoek: Oxford University Press. https://en.wikipedia.org/wiki/Presidency_of_John_Adams. Retrieved: 01/12/2018.

Zack, F. (2017). "Student Loan in America." https://www.forbes.com/sites/zackfriedman/ 2017/04/26/ student-loans-trump/#690ce7e03aa1. Retrieved: 01/28/2018.

Appendix I

List of religions and spiritual traditions around the World
(In Alphabetical Order)

Abrahamic religions

A group of monotheistic traditions sometimes grouped with one another for comparative purposes, because all refer to a patriarch named Abraham. These include:

Bábism

- Azali

Bahá'í Faith

- Bahá'ís Under the Provisions of the Covenant
- Orthodox Bahá'í Faith

Christianity

List of Christian denominations:

Western Christianity
Roman Catholic Church

Protestantism

- Anabaptists (Radical Protestants)
  - o Amish
  - o Hutterites
  - o Mennonites
  - o River Brethren
  - o Schwarzenau Brethren
  - o Shakers

- Anglicanism
  - o Anglo-Catholicism
  - o Broad church
  - o Continuing Anglican movement
  - o English Dissenters (also Nonconformists)
  - o High church
  - o Low church
  - o Open Evangelicals
  - o Puritans
- Baptists
  - o General Baptists (also Free Will Baptists)
  - o Landmarkism
  - o Missionary Baptists
  - o Primitive Baptists
  - o Strict Baptists (also
- Black church
  - o Black theology
- Christian deism and Christian atheism
- Confessing Movement
- Evangelicalism
  - o Charismatic movement
  - o Dispensationalist Christian Zionism
  - o Emerging church
  - o Neo-charismatic movement
  - o Neo-Evangelicalism
  - o Plymouth Brethren
    - ▪ Exclusive Brethren
    - ▪ Open Brethren
  - o Progressive Christianity
  - o Protestant fundamentalism
- Jesuism
- Lutheranism
  - o Pietism
- Methodism
  - o Calvinistic Methodists
  - o Holiness movement
    - ▪ Church of the Nazarene

- o The Salvation Army
- o Wesleyanism
- Pentecostalism
  - o Church of God
  - o Latter Rain movement
  - o Word of Faith
  - o And other New Generation Churches with listless names all over the world
- Proto-Protestant groups:
  - o Hussites
    - ▪ Moravians
  - o Lollardy
  - o Waldensians
- Reformed churches
  - o Amyraldism (called "four-point Calvinism")
  - o Arminianism
    - ▪ Remonstrants
  - o Calvinism
  - o Christian Reconstructionism
  - o Congregational churches
  - o Continental Reformed churches: such as the Swiss Reformed, Dutch Reformed, and French Huguenot churches
  - o Neo-Calvinism
  - o Presbyterianism
  - o Quakers ("Friends")
  - o Zwinglianism
- Restoration movement
  - o Adventism
    - ▪ Branch Davidians
    - ▪ Seventh-day Adventist Church
  - o Christadelphians
  - o Christian Science
  - o Churches of Christ
  - o Iglesia ni Cristo
  - o Jehovah's Witnesses
  - o Latter Day Saint movement

- ▪ Mormon fundamentalism
  - o Millerism
  - o Stone-Campbell movement (called "Campbellites")
- Roman Catholic Church (called Roman Catholicism or "Catholicism"; subsisting predominantly in the Latin Church)
  - o Affirming Catholicism
  - o Breakaway Catholics
  - o Charismatic Catholics
  - o Hebrew Catholics
  - o Independent Catholic churches
    - ▪ Old Catholic Church (Union of Utrecht)
      - ▪ Polish National Catholic Church
  - o Liberal Catholicism
  - o Liberation theology (Latin American Neo-Marxist Catholicism)
  - o Modernist Catholics
  - o Traditionalist Catholics
    - ▪ Sedevacantism
- Unitarianism
- Western esotericism
  - o Behmenism
  - o Christian Kabbalah
  - o Martinism
  - o Rosicrucianism
  - o Swedenborgianism (or "The New Church")

Eastern Christianity

- Church of the East (called "Nestorian")
  - o Ancient Church of the East
  - o Assyrian Church of the East
  - o Chaldean Catholic Church
- Eastern Catholic Churches : In full communion with and subject to the Catholic Communion and Roman Church, but retaining a diverse array of Eastern Christian liturgical rites; including the Maronites and Byzantine Catholics.
- Oriental Orthodox Churches (called Non-Chalcedonian or miaphysite/"monophysite"): Includes the Armenian Apostolic,

Coptic, Syrian Orthodox, Ethiopian and Eritrean Orthodox Churches, as well as a portion of the St. Thomas Christians in India.

- Orthodox Catholic Church (called "Eastern Orthodoxy" or Orthodoxy): Includes the Greek Orthodox, Serbian Orthodox, Russian Orthodox, Romanian Orthodox, Bulgarian Orthodox, Georgian Orthodox, and several other autocephalous and autonomous Churches.
    - o Greek Old Calendarists (called "Genuine Orthodox" or "True Orthodox")
    - o Russian Old Believers (or "Old Ritualists")
        - Bezpopovtsy
        - Popovtsy
- Spiritual Christianity
    - o Doukhobor
    - o Molokan
    - o White Garment Churches

Other Christian

Certain Christian groups are difficult to classify as "Eastern" or "Western."

- Christian Gnosticism
- Christian Universalism
- Nontrinitarianism
- Messianic Judaism
- Rastafari
- Unification Church
- Eastern Lightning

No-longer-extant Christian groups

- Arianism
- Ebionites
- Marcionism

Gnosticism

Many Gnostic groups were closely related to early Christianity, for example, Valentinism. Irenaeus wrote polemics against them from the standpoint of the then-unified Catholic Church.

List of Gnostic sects

- Bosnian Church (no longer extant)
- Cerdonians (no longer extant)
- Colarbasians (no longer extant)
- Simonians (no longer extant)
- Bogomilism (no longer extant)
- Catharism (no longer extant)

The Yazidis are a syncretic Kurdish religion with a Gnostic influence:

- Yazidis

Persian Gnosticism

- Mandaeism
- Manichaeism (no longer extant)
- Bagnolians (no longer extant)

Syrian-Egyptic Gnosticism

None of these religions are still extant.

Syrian-Egyptic Gnosticism

- Sethianism
  - o   Basilideans
  - o   Valentinianism
    - ▪   Bardaisan#Bardesanite school

Neo-Gnostic Groups

- Ecclesia Gnostica
- Ecclesia Gnostica Catholica

Islam

Islamic schools and branches

Kalam (philosophical schools)
Ilm al-Kalam

- Murji'ah
- Mu'tazila

Kharijite
Khawarij

- Azraqi
- Haruriyyah
- Ibadi (only surviving sect)
- Sufri

Shia Islam
Shia Islam

- Bektashi Order
- Isma'ilism
  o Mustaali / Dawoodi Bohra
  o Nizari
- Ja'fari jurisprudence
  o Twelver
    ▪ Akhbari
    ▪ Shaykhism
    ▪ Usuli
  o Alawites
  o Alevism / Bektashi Order
- Ni'matullāhī
- Zaidiyyah

Sufism

- Chishti Order
- Mevlevi Order
- Naqshbandi

- o Jahriyya
- o Khufiyya
- Qadiriyya
- Suhrawardiyya
- Tariqa
- Tijaniyyah

Recent Sufi groups

- Sufi Order International
- Sufism Reoriented
- Universal Sufism
  - o Dances of Universal Peace

Sunni Islam

- Hanafi
  - o Ash'ari
  - o Barelvi
  - o Maturidi
- Hanbali
- Maliki
- Shafi'i
- Wahhabism

Universalist movements

- Xidaotang

Restorationism
Islamism

- Ahl al-Hadith
- Ghair Muqallidism
  - o Deobandi
  - o Yihewani
- Muwahhidism
- Salafi movement
- Wahhabism

Quranism

- Quranism
- Tolu-e-Islam
- United Submitters International

Black Muslims
Black Muslims (disambiguation)

- American Society of Muslims
- Five-Percent Nation
- Moorish Orthodox Church of America
- Moorish Science Temple of America
- Nation of Islam
- United Nation of Islam

Ahmadiyya

- Ahmadiyya Muslim Community
- Lahore Ahmadiyya Movement for the Propagation of Islam

Other Islamic groups

- Al-Fatiha Foundation
- Canadian Muslim Union
- European Islam
- Ittifaq al-Muslimin
- Jadid
- Jamaat al Muslimeen
- Liberal movements within Islam
- Mahdavia
- Muslim Canadian Congress
- Progressive British Muslims
- Progressive Muslim Union
- Riaz Ahmed Gohar Shahi
    o Valentinianism
- Yarsanism

Sufi and Shia Sects

- Alevism
- Bektashi Order
- Moorish Orthodox Church of America

Druze

- Orchonid Druze (in Lebanon, Syria, Israel...)
- Dyayummar Druze (in Lebanon only)
- Messaite Druze (possibly in any place)

Judaism and related religions

Jewish religious movements

Rabbinic Judaism
Rabbinic Judaism

- Conservative (Masorti) Judaism
- Humanistic Judaism (not always identified as a religion)
- Jewish Renewal
- Orthodox Judaism
    - o   Haredi Judaism
    - o   Hasidic Judaism
    - o   Modern Orthodox Judaism
- Reconstructionist Judaism
- Reform Judaism

Karaite Judaism
Karaite Judaism

Samaritanism
Samaritans

Samaritans use a slightly different version of the Pentateuch as their Torah, worshiping at Mount Gerizim instead of Jerusalem, and are possibly the descendants of the lost Northern Kingdom. They are definitely of ancient Israelite origin, but their status as Jews is disputed.

Falasha or Beta Israel
Noahidism

Noahidism is a monotheistic ideology based on the Seven Laws of Noah, and on their traditional interpretations within Rabbinic Judaism. According to Jewish law, non-Jews are not obligated to convert to Judaism, but they are required to observe the Seven Laws of Noah.

Historical groups

Second Temple Judaism

- Essenes
- Pharisees (ancestor of Rabbinic Judaism)
- Sadducees (possible ancestor of Karaite Judaism)
- Zealots (Judea)
    o Sicarii
- Sects that believed Jesus was a prophet
    o Ebionites
    o Elcesaites
    o Nazarenes
- Sabbateans
    o Frankism

Black Hebrew Israelites

Rastafari movement

Rastafari movement

Mandaeans and Sabians

Mandaeism and Sabians

- Mandaeism
- Sabians
    o Mandaean Nasaraean Sabeans
    o Sabians of Harran

Shabakism

Shabak people § Religious beliefs

Indian religions

Indian religions are the religions that originated in the Indian subcontinent; namely Hinduism, Jainism, Buddhism and Sikhism, and religions and traditions related to, and descended from them.

Bhakti movement

- Kabir Panth
- Ravidassia
- Sant Mat
    - Divine Light Mission
    - Eckankar
    - Radhasoami
        - Radha Soami Satsang Beas
        - Radha Swami Satsang, Dinod

Buddhism

Schools of Buddhism

- Nikaya schools (which have historically been incorrectly called Hinayana in the West)
    - Buddha-nature
        - Daśabhūmikā (absorbed into Huayan)
        - Huayan school (*Avataṃsaka*)
            - Hwaeom
            - Kegon
    - Humanistic Buddhism
    - Madhyamaka
        - East Asian Mādhyamaka (Three Treatise school)
        - Jonang
        - Prasangika
        - Svatantrika
    - Nichiren Buddhism

- Nichiren Shōshū
- Nichiren Shū
- Soka Gakkai
  - o Pure Land Buddhism
    - Jōdo Shinshū
    - Jōdo-shū
  - o Theravada
    - Bangladeshi Sangharaj Nikaya
    - Bangladeshi Mahasthabir Nikaya
    - Burmese Dwara Nikaya
    - Burmese Shwegyin Nikaya
    - Burmese Thudhamma Nikaya
      - Vipassana tradition of Mahasi Sayadaw and disciples
    - Sri Lankan Amarapura Nikaya
    - Sri Lankan Ramañña Nikaya
    - Sri Lankan Siam Nikaya
    - Thai Dhammayuttika Nikaya
    - Thai Forest Tradition
    - Tradition of Ajahn Chah
    - Thai Maha Nikaya
    - Dhammakaya Movement
  - o Vipassana movement
- Mahayana
  - o Tiantai
    - Tendai
    - Cheontae
  - o Yogācāra
    - East Asian Yogācāra
  - o Chan Buddhism
    - Caodong school
    - Zen
      - Sōtō
        - Keizan line
        - Jakuen line
        - Giin line
    - Linji school

- Rinzai school
- Ōbaku
- Fuke-shū
- Won Buddhism
  - Kwan Um School of Zen
  - Sanbo Kyodan
- Vajrayana
  - Shingon Buddhism
  - Tibetan Buddhism
    - Bon
    - Gelug
    - Kagyu
      - Dagpo Kagyu
        - Karma Kagyu
        - Barom Kagyu
        - Drukpa Lineage
      - Shangpa Kagyu
    - Nyingma
    - Sakya
    - Jonang
    - Bodongpa
- Navayana
  - Dalit Buddhist movement
- New Buddhist movements
  - Neo-Buddhist movement
  - Shambhala Buddhism
  - Diamond Way Buddhism
  - Triratna Buddhist Community
  - New Kadampa Tradition[10]
  - Share International
  - True Buddha School
    - Nipponzan-Myōhōji-Daisanga
  - Hòa Hảo
- Global variants of Buddhism
  - Buddhism in the United States

Din-e Ilahi

- Din-e Ilahi

Hinduism

Hindu denominations

- Ayyavazhi (sometimes classified as an independent religion)
- Lingayatism
- Shaivism
- Shaktism
- Shrauta
- Smartism
- Swaminarayan
- Tantrism
  - o   Ananda Marga
- Vaishnavism
  - o   Brahma Sampradaya
    - ▪ Gaudiya Vaishnavism
      - ▪ International Society for Krishna Consciousness
    - ▪ Sri Vaishnavism
    - ▪ Rudra Sampradaya
    - ▪ Nimbarka Sampradaya
    - ▪ Varkari Sampradaya
- Hindu reform movements
  - o   Arya Samaj
  - o   Brahmo Samaj
  - o   Ramakrishna Mission
  - o   Satsang of Thakur Anukulchandra
  - o   Satya Dharma
  - o   Matua Mahasangha
- The Osho or Rajneesh movement

Major schools and movements of Hindu philosophy *Hindu philosophy*

- Nyaya
- Purva mimamsa
- Samkhya

- Vaisheshika
- Vedanta (Uttara Mimamsa)
    - o Advaita Vedanta
    - o Integral Yoga
    - o Dvaita Vedanta
    - o Vishishtadvaita
- Yoga
    - o Ashtanga Yoga
    - o Bhakti yoga
    - o Jnana yoga
    - o Karma yoga
    - o Kundalini yoga
    - o Hatha yoga
    - o Raja yoga
    - o Sahaja Yoga
    - o Siddha Yoga
    - o Surat Shabd Yoga
    - o Tantric Yoga

Jainism

- Digambara
    - o Bispanthi
    - o Digambar Terapanth
    - o Kanji Panth
    - o Panth of Kanji Swami
- Śvētāmbara
    - o Murtipujaka (Deravasi)
    - o Sthānakavāsī
    - o Svetambar Terapanth

Meivazhi

- Meivazhi

Sikhism

Sikhism

- Khalsa
  - o   Nihang
- Namdhari ("Kuka Sikhs")
- Ravidassia religion
- Sahajdhari

Iranian religions

Zoroastrianism

- Behafaridians
- Mazdakism
- Zurvanism
- Khurramites (syncretism with Shi'a Islam)

Gnostic religions

- Mandaeism
- Manichaeism
- Mithraism

Bábí movement

- Azali
- Bábism
- Bahá'í Faith

Yazdânism

- Alevi (this is contested; most Alevi consider themselves to be Shia or Sufi Muslims, but a minority adhere to the Yazdani interpretation)
- Yarsani
- Yazidi

East Asian religions

Confucianism

- Neo-Confucianism
- New Confucianism

Shinto

Shinto and Shinto sects and schools

- Koshintō
- Shugendō
- Yoshida Shintō

Shinto-inspired religions

- Konkokyo
- Oomoto
- Seicho-no-Ie
- Shinmeiaishinkai
- Tenrikyo
- Zenrinkyo

Taoism

- Way of the Five Pecks of Rice
  - o   Way of the Celestial Masters
    - ▪ Zhengyi Dao ("Way of the Right Oneness")
- *Taipingjing*-based movements
- Shangqing School ("School of the Highest Clarity")
- Lingbao School ("School of the Numinous Treasure")
- Quanzhen School ("Way of the Fulfilled Virtue")
  - o   Dragon Gate Taoism
- Wuliupai ("School of Wu-Liu")
- Yao Taoism (Meishanism)
- Faism (Redhead Taoism)
- Xuanxue (Neo-Taoism)

Contemporary Taoism-inspired religions

- Yiguandao
- Dudeism (The Church of the Latter-Day Dude)
- Zenarchy (Kerry Wendell Thornley)

Other

Chinese

- Chan Buddhism
- Chinese folk religion
- Falun Gong
- Yiguandao (I Kuan-Tao)
- Mohism
- Xiantiandao

Korean

- Cheondoism
- Daejongism
- Daesun Jinrihoe
- Gasin faith
- Jeung San Do
- Juche
- Korean shamanism
- Won Buddhism
- Suwunism

Vietnamese

- Cao Đài
- Đạo Bửu Sơn Kỳ Hương
- Đạo Dừa

Manchu

- Manchu shamanism

African diasporic religions

African diasporic religions are a number of related religions that developed in the Americas among African slaves and their descendants in various countries of the Caribbean Islands and Latin America, as well as parts of the southern United States. They derive from African traditional religions, especially of West and Central Africa, showing similarities to the Yoruba religion in particular.

- Batuque
- Candomblé
- Dahomey mythology
- Haitian mythology
- Kumina
- Macumba
- Mami Wata
- Obeah
- Oyotunji
- Palo
- Ifa
- Lucumi
- Hudu
- Quimbanda
- Santería (Lukumi)
- Umbanda[15]
- Vodou

Mesoamerican religions

- Aztec religion
- Maya religion
  - o   Lacandon religion
- Mixtec religion
- Olmec religion

- Purepecha religion
- Totonac religion
- Zapotec religion

Indigenous traditional religions

Paganism and Folk religion

Traditionally, these faiths have all been classified "Pagan", but scholars prefer the terms "indigenous/primal/folk/ethnic religions".

African

African traditional religions

Northern Africa

- Berber religion

West Africa

- Akan religion
    o   Ashanti mythology (Ghana)
- Dahomey (Fon) religion
- Bori (Hausa people)
- Efik mythology (Nigeria, Cameroon)
- Serer religion
- Odinani (Nigeria, Cameroon)
- Isoko mythology (Nigeria)
- Yoruba religion (Nigeria, Benin)
- Ifa Afa Fa

Central Africa

- Bushongo mythology (Congo)
- Bambuti (Pygmy) mythology (Congo)
- Lugbara religion (Congo) East Africa
- Akamba mythology (East Kenya)
- Dinka religion (Sudan)
- Lotuko mythology (Sudan)
- Masai mythology (Kenya, Tanzania)

- Malagasy mythology
- Oromo religion (Ethiopia) Southern Africa
- Badimo (Botswana)
- Khoisan religion
- Lozi mythology (Zambia)
- Tumbuka mythology (Malawi)
- Zulu religion (South Africa)

American

Native American mythology

North American

- Abenaki mythology
- Anishinaabe
- Blackfoot mythology
- Cherokee mythology
- Chickasaw mythology
- Choctaw mythology
- Creek mythology
- Crow mythology
- Haida mythology
- Ho-Chunk mythology (aka: Winnebago)
- Hopi mythology
- Inuit mythology
- Iroquois mythology
- Keetoowah Nighthawk Society
- Kuksu
- Kwakiutl mythology
- Lakota mythology
- Leni Lenape mythology
- Longhouse religion
- Midewiwin
- Miwok
- Navajo mythology
- Nootka mythology
- Ohlone mythology
- Pomo mythology

- Pawnee mythology
- Salish mythology
- Selk'nam religion
- Seneca mythology
- Southeastern Ceremonial Complex
- Sun Dance
- Tsimshian mythology
- Urarina
- Ute mythology
- Wyandot religion
- Zuni mythology

South American

- Guarani mythology
- Inca mythology
- Jivaroan religion
- Mapuche religion
- Muisca religion and Muisca mythology

Eurasian

Asian

- Bathouism
- Benzhuism (indigenous religion of the Bai people)
- Bimoism (indigenous religion of the Yi people)
- Bon
- Chinese mythology
- Japanese mythology
- Korean shamanism
- Manchu shamanism
- Mun (Lepcha)
- Pemena (Karo people (Indonesia))
- Shamanism in Siberia
- Tengrism
- Ua Dab (indigenous religion of the Hmong people)
- Vietnamese folk religion European

- Estonian mythology
- Shamanism among Eskimo peoples
- Finnish mythology and Finnish paganism
- Shamanistic remnants in Hungarian folklore
- Sami shamanism

Oceania/Pacific/Maritime Southeast Asia

- Australian Aboriginal mythology (Dreamtime)
- Austronesian beliefs
  - o Indonesian mythology
    - Aluk Todolo (indigenous religion of the Toraja people)
    - Balinese mythology
      - Balinese Hinduism
    - Traditional Batak religion
      - Parmalim
    - Kaharingan (indigenous religion of the Dayak people)
    - Javanese beliefs
    - Marapu (indigenous religion of the Sumba people)
    - Pemena (indigenous religion of the Karo people)
    - Sunda Wiwitan (indigenous religion of the Sundanese people)
  - o Melanesian mythology
  - o Micronesian mythology
    - Modekngei
    - Nauruan indigenous religion
  - o Philippine indigenous religions
    - Tagalog indigenous religion
    - Tagbanwa indigenous religion
  - o Polynesian mythology
    - Cook Islands mythology
    - Hawaiian mythology
    - Māori mythology
    - Māori religion

- Pai Mārire
- Rātana
- Ringatū
- Rapa Nui mythology
- Moai
- Tangata manu

Cargo cults

- John Frum
- Johnson cult
- Prince Philip Movement
- Vailala Madness

Historical religions

Prehistoric religion and History of religion

Most historical religions were polytheistic, but some, such as Atenism, were much closer to monotheism.

Ancient Near Eastern

Ancient Near Eastern religions

- Ancient Egyptian religion
  - o Atenism
- Ancient Semitic religion
  - o Ancient Canaanite religion
    - Religion in Carthage
    - Palmyrene religion
  - o Ancient Mesopotamian religion
    - Babylonian and Assyrian religion
    - Babylonian religion
    - Chaldean mythology
    - Sumerian religion
  - o Religion in pre-Islamic Arabia
    - Nabataean religion

Indo-European

Proto-Indo-European religion

- Proto-Indo-Iranian religion
    - o   Historical Vedic religion
    - o   Iranian mythology
- Armenian mythology
- Baltic polytheism
- Celtic polytheism
- Germanic paganism
    - o   Anglo-Saxon paganism
    - o   Continental Germanic mythology
    - o   Norse religion
- Greek polytheism
- Hittite mythology
- Persian mythology
- Religion in ancient Rome
- Slavic mythology

Hellenistic

Hellenistic religion

- Gallo-Roman religion
- Glycon cult
- Mystery religions
    - o   Eleusinian Mysteries
    - o   Mithraic mysteries
    - o   Orphism
- Pythagoreanism

Uralic

- Estonian polytheism
- Finnish polytheism
- Hungarian polytheism

Mysticism and occult

Esotericism and mysticism

- Anthroposophy
- Buddhist esoteric tradition
- Hindu mysticism
    o Tantra
- • Kabbalah
    o Christian Kabbalah
- Neoplatonism
- Pythagoreanism
    o Neopythagoreanism
- Sufism
- Theosophy

Western mystery tradition

Esoteric Christianity, Christian mysticism, Jewish mysticism, and Islamic mysticism

- Archeosophical Society
- Behmenism
- Builders of the Adytum
- Fraternitas Saturni
- Fraternity of the Inner Light
- Hermetic Order of the Golden Dawn
    o The Open Source Order of the Golden Dawn
- Hermeticism
- Martinism
- Ordo Aurum Solis
- Rosicrucian
    o Ancient Mystical Order Rosae Crucis
    o Rosicrucian Fellowship
- Servants of the Light
- Thelema
    o A∴A∴

- o Ordo Templi Orientis
- o Typhonian Order

Occult and magic

Occult § Occultism, and Magic (paranormal)

- Alchemy
- Ceremonial magic
  - o Enochian magic
  - o Goetia
- Chaos magic
  - o Illuminates of Thanateros
  - o Thee Temple ov Psychick Youth
- Hoodoo (folk magic) (Rootwork)
  - o Louisiana Voodoo
- Kulam – Filipino witchcraft
- Pow-wow (folk magic)
- Magick (Thelema)
- Contemporary witchcraft

Modern paganism

List of Neopagan movements

Syncretic

- Adonism
- Church of All Worlds
- Church of Aphrodite
- Feraferia
- Koshintō
- Neo-Druidism
  - o Ár nDraíocht Féin
  - o Order of Bards, Ovates, and Druids
  - o Reformed Druids of North America
- Neoshamanism
- Neo-völkisch movements

- Technopaganism
- Wicca
  - o British Traditional Wicca
    - Gardnerian Wicca
    - Alexandrian Wicca
    - Central Valley Wicca
    - Algard Wicca
    - Chthonioi Alexandrian Wicca
    - Blue Star Wicca
  - o Seax-Wica
  - o Universal Eclectic Wicca
  - o Celtic Wicca
  - o Dianic Wicca
  - o Faery Wicca
  - o Feri Tradition
  - o Georgian Wicca
  - o Odyssean Wicca
  - o Wiccan church
    - Covenant of the Goddess

Ethnic

Ethnic religion

- Armenian neopaganism
- Baltic neopaganism
- Celtic neopaganism
- Dievturība
- Estonian neopaganism
- Finnish neopaganism
- Germanic neopaganism
- Hellenism (religion)
- Italo-Roman neopaganism
- Kemetism
- Mari native religion
- Odinism
- Romuva (religion)
- Semitic neopaganism

- Slavic neopaganism
- Wotanism
- Zalmoxianism

New religious movements

List of new religious movements

- Eckankar
- Huna
- Omnism
- Raëlism
- Scientology
- Unitarian Universalism

Race-based

Ethnic religion

Black

- Ausar Auset Society
- Black Hebrew Israelites
- Dini Ya Msambwa
- Mumboism
- Nation of Gods and Earths
- Nation of Islam
- Nuwaubian Nation
- Moorish Orthodox Church of America
- Moorish Science Temple of America
- Rastafari

White

- Ariosophy
- Black Order (Satanist group)
- Christian Identity
- Creativity

- Order of Nine Angles
- Thule Society
- Wotansvolk

Native American

- Ghost Dance
- Indian Shaker Church
- Native American Church

New Thought

New Thought

- Christian Science
- Church of Divine Science
- Church Universal and Triumphant
- Religious Science
- Unity Church
- Jewish Science
- Seicho-no-Ie

Shinshukyo

Japanese new religions

- Church of World Messianity
- Happy Science
- Konkokyo
- Oomoto
- PL Kyodan
- Seicho-no-Ie
- Tenrikyo

Left-hand path religions

Left-hand path and right-hand path

- Demonolatry
- Luciferianism
- Satanism
    - o   LaVeyan Satanism
    - o   Theistic Satanism
        - ▪ Our Lady of Endor Coven (or Ophite Cultus Satanas)
- Temple of Set

Post-theistic and naturalistic religions

- Creativity (religion)
- Discordianism
- Ethical movement
- Freethought
    - o   North Texas Church of Freethought
- Jediism
- Moorish Orthodox Church of America
- Naturalistic pantheism
    - o   World Pantheist Movement
- Religion of Humanity
- Syntheism

Others

- The Circle of Reason
- Cult of Reason (1792–1794)
- Cult of the Supreme Being
- Deism
- Fourth Way
- God-Building
- Goddess movement
- Humanism
- Open-source religion

- Spiritism (Spiritualism)
- Subud
- Universal Life Church

Parody or mock religions

- Church of Euthanasia
- The Church of the Flying Spaghetti Monster
- Church of the SubGenius
- Dinkoism
- Dudeism
- Iglesia Maradoniana
- Invisible Pink Unicorn
- Kibology
- Kopimism
- Landover Baptist Church
- Last Thursdayism
- Cult of Kek

(Source: https://en.wikipedia.org/wiki/List_of_religions_and_spiritual_traditions)

www.ingramcontent.com/pod-product-compliance
Lightning Source LLC
Chambersburg PA
CBHW052114030426
42335CB00025B/2978